D1557397

The other Puerto Rico

Kathryn Robinson

Published by Permanent Press Inc.

The Other Puerto Rico

Copyright© Kathryn Robinson 1984

All rights reserved
Published in 1984 by Permanent Press, Inc.
Calle San Mateo 1614, Santurce, Puerto Rico-USA 00912

Second edition: 1992 Fifth printing: 1992
Library of Congress Catalog Card Number F1965.3R63 1984,
917.295'0453 84-1040
ISBN 0-915393-19-0

Portions of this book originally appeared in
The San Juan Star, Sunday Magazine
Printed in the United States of America
Designed by Miguel Vélez

Color photographs not specifically credited
were taken by John Harmon.

Black and white photographs not specifically
credited were taken by the author.

*For
Louisa
and
James
Robinson*

Preface to the Third Edition

Since the publication of **The Other Puerto Rico** in 1984, my attentions have turned to other projects and to two young daughters. The book, for its part, seems to have taken on a life of its own. It has been reprinted three times and, somewhat to my surprise, continues to elicit enthusiastic comments from people who have read it. Once again, my publisher and I are extending the book's life. In this new edition, the text has been left untouched with the exception of a few minor time changes. At the end of each chapter, the If You Go section has been replaced with a 1990s Update for which I have investigated the current status of places mentioned in the text. In this way, the flavor of the original book is retained, yet the book is more useful to today's visitors. In order to add current information, I have eliminated most road directions; with a detailed highway map and a few creative guesses, drivers will reach their destinations. I have also eliminated most lodging and restaurants not mentioned in the text; **Qué Pasa** or another local tourism magazine can provide more accurate information. A special thanks goes to the people at the Department of Natural Resources, who generously answered my many questions about the forests.

In the original foreword, I mentioned a hope that, a century from then, most of the places in the book would still be able to provide others with the same enjoyment they gave me. Almost one-tenth of the way into that century, the places remain basically unchanged, and increasing concern for the island's natural resources bodes well for their continued existence.

The Other Puerto Rico

Kathryn Robinson

TABLE OF CONTENTS

Botanical Garden (photo by John Harmon)

SAN JUAN'S GARDEN OF TROPICAL DELIGHTS

Have you ever seen a monkey's ear, a cannonball, a sausage, a green pouch, a yellow candle — all dangling from trees? Have you ever sat under a six-foot-wide mushroom and peered at wrinkled skins, tiger faces and scorpion bodies in an orchid garden? Have you ever felt like a shrunken Alice in a wonderland of massive roots, towering palm trunks, sprouting banana leaf fans, or 90-foot trees wrapped in vines? If you have not, then you have never visited the Botanical Garden at the University of Puerto Rico Agricultural Experiment Station in Río Piedras.

Background

The Botanical Garden was opened in 1969 to provide a setting for tropical and subtropical vegetation in the heart of metropolitan San Juan. Over 200 species of trees, bushes and plants mingle in areas bordered by lagoons, small waterfalls, shelters and a series of paths. Forty acres have been landscaped, but that is only the beginning: plans already exist to develop the remaining 140 acres in stages, depending on available money. Recreation, culture, education and science combine in the objectives of the garden. Visitors wander along shady, breezy paths as they learn to appreciate flora in natural settings and to identify numerous native and introduced species found in Puerto Rico. At the same time, the center preserves native vegetation and provide a genetic bank for studies of tropical flora.

Several stately turn-of-the-century buildings on the grounds house, among other institutions, the Agricultural Experiment Station and the Institute of Tropical Forestry. The Experiment Station, part of the University of Puerto Rico at Mayagüez; works with six substations scattered around the island in studies related to agriculture, agronomy and plant pathology. Its agricultural library is considered one of the best in the Caribbean. The Institute of Tropical Forestry, part of the U.S. Forest Service, conducts research on tropical tree and wildlife species. Its library is said to be the largest on tropical forestry in this hemisphere. Both libraries are open to the public during the week.

A. *Tree sculpture along the main path* B. *Leaves with bark* C. *Aerial roots of the banyan*

Wandering through the gardens

Once visitors enter the Botanical Garden, Río Piedras's noises become muffled and insignificant. Gravel paths — gradual and well maintained — fan out in several directions between "cliffs" of tangled plants, vines and leaves, mixed with occasional bright flowers. Markers identify some of the vegetation. In several especially lush spots, visitors can imagine themselves part of Aguirre's lost band of Amazon explorers.

The main path makes an elongated loop around a pond of murky water and lavender water lilies. Plants bordering the path press together. There are the "elephant-ear" leaves of **yautía**, "Swiss-cheese" leaves of philodendron, "tiger-spotted" leaves of snake plants and "lobster" claws of heliconia. Asparagus ferns, white Bengal clockvines and heather blossoms cloak many trees.

Tropical vegetation seems to outdo that of more temperate climates both in lushness and in creativity. One cluster of dracaena bushes resembles camels at water. Yellow nuts grow at the top of the thin trunk of a betel nut palm. Senegal date palm plumes look like exploding firecrackers. A candle tree grows close to the ground; long waxy yellow fruit hang from its branches. At the top of a cannonball tree are its leaves; below, dung-colored cannonball fruit dangle next to sweet-smelling flowers. A side path penetrates a 30-foot-high mesh of roots, spiked branches and serrated leaves. There are also quinine trees, starry gardenias and an Australian punk tree as well as the more commonly seen breadfruits, Indian almonds and African tulip trees. Less noticeable are the trees and bushes which produce bay rum, chocolate, cinnamon, cloves, nutmeg and other spices. All are representative of flora found in the tropics and subtropics.

Above the main path, canopies of bamboo stems and their feathery foliage lead visitors to an open A-frame chapel and wooden tables and benches, reportedly the site of many weddings. At the far end of the pond another path parallels a stream and skirts two manmade ponds. A small pier extending into the larger one offers a close look at paddling ducks and geese. Shaded benches bordering the water invite visitors to sit and daydream.

The orchid garden next to the ponds is perhaps the favorite section of the Botanical Garden. Several species of vanda orchids, which flourish in the sun, are placed in widely spaced rows for easy viewing. Large floppy flowers and neat miniatures come in tones of lilac, peach, white, yellow and sepia. The plants climb stumps, trellises or pebble beds lined with coconut fiber. The tired visitor can rest on a bench under a giant mushroom-shaped shelter in one corner and feel like a character from a fanciful children's book. Most of the Botanical Garden's 30,000 orchids, of which there are both small native species and showy hybrid types, need shade and are grown in a separate area accessible only by special appointment.

Spacious, well tended lawns surround the orchid garden. Shaded benches have been placed on a hill near restrooms and log bases which spout drinking water. A pavillion houses some of the more exotic plants and orchids.

A monkey-ear tree, native to Venezuela, sprawls above one slope. Spreading gray branches that support clusters of tiny leaves give the tree its huge fan shape. Brown ear-shaped seed pods often decorate the tree and the ground beneath. According to a marker next to the tree, its seeds can be made into necklaces, its wood into boats, its bark into soap or medicine and its pods can be eaten. Many of the plants and trees on the grounds are similarly versatile.

Nature seems very solicitous in the Botanical Garden. Shrubs and trees shield visitors from the sun. When we were there, a natural awning covered us during a downpour: we were able to watch the rain, examine a lizard doing "pushups," listen to birds and frogs, and emerge relatively dry when the deluge stopped. Later, a **mamey** fruit dropped almost on top of us; rather than let it rot, we ate it. According to Silverio Medina, Director of the Botanical Garden, eating fruit which has dropped is forgivable, but none may be picked, and no roots may be pulled.

In addition to the orchid garden, Medina mentioned that the Botanical Garden now has a newly completed palm garden, to the left of the main entrance, containing some 125 palm species from Puerto Rico and other countries; at this moment specimens are little more than head high. A fern garden will be opening in the near future. There are also plans for an amphitheater, a garden of plants used to make beverages, another garden for poisonous plants, and terraces of shrubs including hibiscus.

One of the nicest qualities of the garden is its intimate feeling. As we walked through the jungly tangle along the main path, we felt it was **our** jungle. A young couple sat close together on one of the pond benches; for the moment, it was **their** pond. Another couple wandered through the orchids; their children dashed across the lawns in enthusiastic abandon. Two older women sat in the chapel under the bamboo, rarely speaking, as if sitting in their backyards. Visitors quickly find their own private nooks.

1990s UPDATE: Closed following Hurricane Hugo, the garden (763-4409) is once again open daily from 9:00 a.m. to 5:00 p.m. Some 75 acres have now been landscaped, and the young palms have grown considerably. Several directors have come after Medina; the current one is Juan Muñoz. Plans for gardens of ferns and beverage plants have been replaced by plants for arboretums containing native and international plants, and a new garden in homage to Claude Monet has opened. To reach the garden, turn south (right if coming from Las Américas Expressway) into a woodsy area at the intersection of Highways 1 and 3 in Río Piedras. The sign for the entrance is slightly hidden; remain alert or you will miss it. Picnics are permitted on the grounds, but alcoholic beverages or fires of any sort are not.

THE DAYTIME PLEASURES
OF PIÑONES

The beach was deserted. A lone pair of footprints alluded to another person who was no longer there. Ochre-colored sand curved away from a rocky point covered with sparse vegetation. The sea resembled glass and turquoise. The sky, a paler blue, was spotted with puffy clouds and swooping pelicans. Coconut palms and almond trees shaded the beach. Several Australian pine trees stretched toward the sky. Seagrapes and vines patterned the sand. A continual breeze softened the bright sun.

Is this beach some hidden cove in Hawaii, or the South Pacific, or some luxury islet in the Caribbean? No: the advantage of this beach, called Vacia Talega, is that it is a mere half-hour drive from San Juan, just east of Isla Verde.

Vacia Talega is only one of many interesting features of Piñones, the sparsely inhabited coastal area between Boca de Cangrejos and the town of Loíza. Though many local residents think of late-night "parking" and other surreptitious acts when they think of Piñones (and it does seem a place to avoid after sundown), the area offers a diversity of natural pleasures to the daytime visitor.

A drive along the coast

The drive begins at Boca de Cangrejos, a point which somewhat resembles a crab **(cangrejo)** walking out to sea and does harbor live crabs. A cluster of shacks provides drinks and traditional island snacks for those who want to admire San Juan's skyline from a distance. When conditions are right, fishermen walk toward a jagged rock offshore to fish and surfers paddle to waves beyond the rock. Less adventurous fishermen dangle lines from the bridge next to the Boca de Cangrejos Yacht Club. At La Lancha Paseadora, a launch regularly circles the Torrecilla lagoon and the nearby sea.

The Piñones road is initially lined with additional food and drink shacks. A lovely half-moon bay arcs into a promontory. This area becomes jammed on weekends; for those searching for a beach with few footprints, it is best to push on. Soon the food shacks thin out and sand sweeps across the road. Here the beach is more desolate: there are no trees on the ocean side of the road, reef separates sea from sand and tall Australian pine trees (apparently the reason for the name, Piñones) look straggly and dusty. Yet even this stretch becomes crowded on weekends.

A. *Beach day, Piñones* B. *Laguna de Piñones* C. *Ferry across the Río Loíza*

Picnic tables and natural pools attract families with children. Beyond, seagrapes, almond trees and numerous coconut palms begin to replace the pines. Abandoned cars rusting along the road form several makeshift seawalls against the sea.

About a mile and a half from Boca de Cangrejos is a popular surfing beach called Aviones. A reef immediately off its shore makes Aviones strictly for surfers who know how to steer. It has the best and most consistent waves in the San Juan area, and on many weekends the road is crowded with cars and tanned, bleached young people. For novice surfers another beach east of Aviones called Tocones is said to have a sandy bottom. This area is "downtown" Piñones, a cluster of wood and cement houses, bars and a school.

Coconut country begins on the other side of Piñones. There are fields of coconuts — long rows of gray trunks and tangles of feathery plumes high in the air. At one time both coconuts and sugar cane were cultivated here, but only the coconuts remain. Houses are isolated. Most are of weathered wood, set on stilts, with louvered windows and galvanized or tarpapered roofs. Yards are neatly brushed and enclosed by stick and barbed wire fences or tall, spiked cacti that resemble women doubled over in especially tight corsets.

In one yard, we saw a man washing clothes beside the house. In another a woman gracefully followed a herd of cattle into a field. In a third four children played on a makeshift seesaw. The blackness of their skins contrasted with the bright-colored shirts and dresses they were wearing. Parallel to this rural scene is an unbroken strip of beach called Playa de las Tres Palmitas, although here we found many more than three little palms.

Vacia Talega

Vacia Talega bay extends almost up to the road. The beach, semi-deserted during the week, crowded on weekends, has something for everyone. Its firm, flat sand provides a track with a view for joggers and the ideal material for beach sculptors. The ocean floor is free of rocks. Swimmers bathe in almost motionless water next to a promontory, which is actually a group of ancient barrier sand dunes which were cemented together during Pleistocene glaciations. At the tip of the promontory a grassy field, low-lying seagrapes and toothy rock accepting the brunt of incessant waves produce a scene of stark beauty. Away from the point the water is slightly choppier, and a sandy spit points to a small coral reef for amateur snorkelers. Those with stamina and experience (and perhaps a boat or raft) can visit a larger reef about a quarter mile out in the bay.

Fishermen survey miles of undulating shoreline from the dune rock while they wait for a nibble. The more energetic can hike what the fishermen see — six miles of almost continuous beach back to Boca de Cangrejos. Beachcombers find sea fans, coconut bottoms with their shriveled "heads", almond seeds, a variety of shells (depending on the

A. *View toward Vacia Talega* B. *Camera-shy land crab* C. *Road through coconut grove* D. *Frying snack Boca de Cangrejos* E. *San Patrico church, Loíza*

time of year) and small forms of sealife in the flat reefs and rocks close to shore.

Many visitors enjoy picnics or barbecues on the shady fringes of the beach, although there are no facilities here. Everything must be brought in, and taken out. Insect repellent is very welcome in the late afternoon.

Toward Loíza

The road continues another mile and a half, past more dune rocks undercut by the sea, through an awning of dry vegetation, to the Río Loíza. Until the new bridge was built, cars lined up here to be taken across the wide, gentle river in a hand-pulled barge. Some eight cars fit on the flat-bottomed ferry, which men then pulled across the river using a simple system of ropes and guide rollers. A tiny shack served cold drinks to waiting passengers, and on busy days women walked down the road vending delicious coconut cookies, coconut-and-sweet-potato bars and other local snacks. Across the river is the town of Loíza, which has one of the highest percentages of African descendants of any island town and still maintains traditional customs such as performing **bomba y plena** music and dances, crafting coconut **vejigante** masks and preparing land crab dishes and other typical foods. Its San Patricio church is the oldest on the island still actively functioning as a parish church.

On our first visit we did not cross the river, remaining istead on its Piñones side. Across the slow-moving Loíza, wooden houses painted in bright though sun-faded colors are clustered on its banks. Lush peaks of the Sierra de Luquillo upriver contrast with shadowy sandbars next to the ocean. Near where we stood, a young muscular boy, the color of ebony, extended his hand to a large-boned woman in a close-fitting cotton dress, and guided her into his little wooden boat. He slowly, silently rowed the boat across the water. In that moment this area seemed part of another world, a world of another century and another continent.

Lagoons and other natural resources

On the landward side of the road there is a third world, a natural world of lagoons, salt ponds and mangrove forests which constitute the Piñones Forest Reserve. A road identified by a sign near the Piñones school leads into the reserve. At its entrance a boathouse which appears abandoned sits in the water at the edge of Laguna de Piñones. A trail beyond a rustic picnic area winds through mangrove forest bordering the lagoon, as does a dirt road. Thousands of small land crabs with bulging eyes scuttle off the road at the approach of humans, giving credence to the sign informing us that the area is a crab sanctuary.

There are other distinctive aspects to the reserve. Laguna de Piñones contains a large population of bioluminescent microorganisms which give off a phosphorescent glow in the water on dark nights. Some of the few remaining stands of pure pterocarpus **(palo de pollo)** forest in

Puerto Rico grow in a freshwater swamp here. With enormous narrow buttress roots, the tree looks every bit as haunting as its common English name — swamp bloodwood — would suggest. Several lagoons, of which Laguna La Torrecilla is the largest, support some 40 species of fish and even more bird species, including herons, pelicans and the largest population of snowy egrets **(garza blanca)** on the island. The main reason for this great gathering of fish and fowl is the extensive mangrove forest surrounding the lagoons.

Most everything you may have wanted to know about mangroves

Mangroves rim the lagoons and grow on islets in the water at Piñones. They are twisted, shadowy trees, resembling stooped witches or botanical hunchbacks. Dense pencil-like roots rise up to meet aerial roots dangling in search of water. Leaves are small and elliptical. Inner trunks shoot up while outer ones twist themselves into intricate tangles close to the ground. The ground is a drab collection of sediments, leaf litter, salt and evaporating water.

At one time I thought of mangroves as merely desolate breeding grounds for mosquitoes or snarled obstacles in getting to the ocean. This negative impression was altered after an enthusiastic mini-lecture given by a student of mangroves while we were at another reserve. These trees still look scraggly, but I now have respect for their importance in the scheme of coastal ecology.

Piñones contains Puerto Rico's largest remaining mangrove forest, and its largest estuarine zone, which is a mingling of fresh and sea water. The fresh water run-off mixing with the sea, as well as shuttling tides, stimulates the high level of plant and animal productivity found here.

The role of a typical mangrove in the well-programmed scheme of nature is as interesting as it is educational. Red mangroves, for example, are one of the few plants which retain their seeds until they germinate. These seeds are the slender tapers which wash up on beaches in Puerto Rico. They are capable of floating for several months until they drift into land and set down roots.

From the roots come stems and from the stems come leaves. The leaves eventually fall into the bay and are broken down by tiny organisms. Once decomposed, they also provide food for other barely visible animals, including shrimp larvae. The shrimp feed little fish which nourish bigger ones; the cycle continues up to man, the top carnivore.

Mangroves provide a natural habitat for birds. Fish lay eggs and try out their fins among the protective roots. According to more mystical experts, mangroves "walk" into the water. Actually, the roots thrust into the soil on their seaward side, trapping sediment and protecting the coastline from hurricanes or beach erosion.

Landfill placed for homes or other construction in areas such as Piñones impedes the runoff of fresh water. No fresh water means no estuarine balance which means no mangroves which means an eroding coastline. For this reason ecologists bemoan the destruction of mangroves, including the once prevalent custom of chopping them down to make charcoal and fence posts. Nevertheless, it was because of Piñones' importance as one source of posts, charcoal wood and tannin that around 1920 it was declared a forest reserve, placing the cutting of trees under government control.

Those who think, as I did, that if you've seen one mangrove you've seen them all should know there are actually four types in the Piñones reserve. The "reds" stretch farthest into the water; they are known by their hanging aerial roots and stilt roots which look like fingers on a stiffened hand. The "blacks" grow in depressed areas closer to land and are identified by salty-tasting leaves and dark, rough bark. The "whites" spread out on higher land (the highest point in this reserve is three feet above sea level) and salt flats. They have a smooth gray trunk and leathery leaves. Buttonwood mangroves fringe the saline swamp with spreading trees bearing red-brown button-like fruits. Because of a high amount of rainfall, the mangrove trunks on the north coast are denser and shorter than their southern counterparts.

As we left the estuarine zone in the shadowy light of late afternoon, I turned to get one last look at a newly appreciated mangrove tree...and could swear I saw its gnarled stilt roots inching just a little bit farther as it "stepped" into the sea.

1990s UPDATE: Road 187 connects Isla Verde with Boca de Cangrejos and becomes the Piñones road. In the past few years, a number of more solid concrete restaurants have replaced some of the shacks in the area. The road itself, once of hard-packed sand, is now completely paved, and, with the completion of the bridge across the Río Loíza, provides a speedy route to the town of Loíza. On the other hand, another form of progress, a vast development around Vacia Talega which would have destroyed much mangrove forest, has once again been defeated in court. Tourism boats plying the waters of Laguna La Torrecilla and Río Loíza seem to have disappeared, but canoes can be borrowed from the ranger station at Piñones Forest (791-7750). To find out about other mangrove forests, see the Karst Country article. Loíza coconut masks are still sold in a small shop on Road 187, Km. 6.6.

A NOTE ABOUT ISLAND CRAFTS: In the same way that Loíza produces coconut **vejigante** masks, several other island town focus on traditional crafts. For examples, papier-mache carnival masks are fashioned in Ponce, **mundillo** lace in Moca, **cuatros** (guitarlike instruments) in Utuado and animal wood carvings in Jayuya. If you are interested in combining a visit to an island town with a visit to a craft shop, contact the artisan office at the Tourism Company (721-2400) or the Institute of Puerto Rican Culture popular art center on Cristo Street (722-0621).

A. *Foot bridge over the Espíritu Santo* B. *Pool, upper Espíritu Santo* C. *Heliconia* D. *Termite nest in mangro* E. *Catching river shrimp*

DOWN THE ESPIRITU SANTO

Forests and pastures, bamboo and grasses, hyacinths and mangroves, construction and controversy line the Río Espíritu Santo, known as Puerto Rico's only navigable river, which begins in the Sierra de Luquillo, becomes navigable near Highway 3 and empties into the Atlantic Ocean. Its course can be surveyed in an instant by plane, in an hour and a half by launch, and in the better part of a day by canoe. We opted for the canoe trip.

Embarkation

Our embarkation point was the ramp of La Lancha Paseadora in Río Grande. We flipped the canoe off the car, slipped it into the water and stocked it with wooden paddles, life jackets doubling as cushions, canned drinks and beachgear.

The immediate view of bulldozed swaths surrounding slow, turbid water was disheartening. But the canoeing movements — paddles vertical in the water, horizontal when on top — soon lulled us into good spirits. When we slipped silently, smoothly under the massive Highway 3 bridge on our journey upriver, canoes and rivers seemed far superior to cars and highways.

Construction and controversy

Rocks lying just below the surface of the 40-foot-wide, yard-deep river occasionally scraped the canoe with a fingernails-on-blackboard intensity. Five feet above us, a white cloth hanging from a branch marked the high water line. Dense vegetation including mangoes, Indian almonds, flamboyants and bamboo crowd the river banks. Weeds encroach on an abandoned bridge piling. Long-necked green herons **(martinete)** skirted the water, and a woodpecker **(carpintero)** sentried from a tree. Orange-roofed feed hoppers identify a chicken farm. Boulder and cattle-studded pastures cover the hills.

This pastoral scene was unexpectedly interrupted by a ten-foot-high dam. The dam (and construction of a filtration plant opposite the ramp which we had seen earlier) is the first phase of the controversial El Yunque water supply project. Proponents of the dam project argue that Puerto Rico will soon need the additional water. Opponents counter that the proposed reservoir would kill many forms of aquatic life that must annually migrate from upstream to the sea, submerge Indian rock carvings, and flood a toxic garbage dump, and point out that alternatives for water exist.

21

Completion of the first phase undoubtedly pleases dam proponents, lovers of the leveled-land look of progress, and neighborhood youth, who ignore the "Swimming is Prohibited" signs. On the other hand, it dismays canoeists and admirers of river shrimp.

The plight of the river shrimp

In the folds of the mountains, long before the Espíritu Santo becomes navigable, the river rushes over boulders and debris into pools containing numerous river shrimp, some a foot long. A coffee plantation until 75 years ago, this area is now a jungly part of the Caribbean National Forest.

The river shrimp crawling on submerged rocks were originally saltwater animals. They adapted to freshwater, evolving claws similar to those of Maine lobsters, yet must still return to the brackish mouth of the river during their larva stage. When floods hit, the larvae descend to the river bed to avoid being swept to sea. They are an important source of food for fish here — a low rung in the food ladder.

After 50 days in the estuaries, those not swept to sea or martyred to the food chain congregate and swim upriver. If there is an obstacle, usually a waterfall, they leave the water and climb rocks, staying near the spray so their gills do not dry out. However, if the obstacle is too great, the shrimp —and several fish species including the small olivo **(cetí)**— cannot complete their cycle and soon vanish from the river.

River shrimp have long been a popular food on the island; some prefer its delicate taste to that of lobster. Traditional methods of catching the shrimp range from placing bait on the wrist and grabbing the crustacean when it approaches, to lassoing its body with a vine and stick contraption. Common baits are codfish, chicken entrails and coconut. Modern devices include nets resembling those used to catch butterflies and cylindrical traps left in the water overnight, when the shrimp usually venture out.

Unfortunately, as more rivers on the island are dammed to form reservoirs, fewer river shrimp are able to complete their pilgrimages to the sea, and **camarones del río** become an expensive delicacy for some, a meal relegated to memory for others.

Continuing upriver

Somewhat stubbornly, we skirted the dam, portaging the canoe up a 30-foot embankment and across more bulldozed land to an accessible launching site. Here the water level is considerably higher, and several mango trees seem to be wading in the river. Pastures and forest patches dwarf isolated homes and a strange grouping of brightly painted boulders, which are in turn dwarfed by the distant Sierra de Luquillo.

Although the mountains seemed to beckon us closer, the water became clearer and shallower. Rocks poking out of the river served as steppingstones for a family of picnickers but as a natural barrier for us. We retraced the mile of river to the ramp and continued on the more easily navigated five miles of waterway to the sea.

Downriver

After passing a casual riverside restaurant and an unmoored clump of bamboo foundering in the river, we found the atmosphere harsher. Early afternoon sun scorched from a cloudless sky. Leaning bamboo shaded only the immediate banks. Flat fields of grass replace forest and hilly pastures. The river, deeper and wider now, was clouded with sediment and organic matter. A red-tailed hawk **(guaraguao)** circled overhead.

A box-shaped, fringe-roofed launch, named La Viticuev but better known as La Paseadora, motored by us several times as we paddled to sea. Its passengers peered curiously or waved; the wake gently rocked our canoe. More rambunctious passengers in smaller motorboats warhooped or shouted "Indios! Indios!" at our approach. We must have looked like American Indians somehow transposed into an African grasslands setting with Kilimanjaro in the background.

The estuary

One or two bends in the river later, small patches of water hyacinths massed along the banks. Hyacinths grow best where nutrient levels are high; their dangling roots absorb fertilizers. Tall, brown-edged ferns crowded together in open, sunny patches on land. Soon this vegetation gives way to the tangled labyrinths of mangrove forest. Four types of mangroves (buttonwood, black, white and red, which is most visible here) coexist with buttressing pterocarpus **(palo de pollo)** trees. Pods hang like drop earrings from mangrove branches; prop roots form unruly scaffolds as they edge into the water. Rich mangrove smells mingled with the odor of gasoline from boats.

As in all estuarine zones, the animal life here is abundant. Shuttling tides and mingling fresh and seawater produce a high level of plant and animal productivity. We saw hundreds of red crabs scuttle along roots. A mongoose paddled in great haste across the river. Anxious fish jumped out of the water when they sensed us. Anis **(judío)** and pelicans branch-hopped in the mangroves. Termites abounded in bulging nests.

Two or three side channels seemed intriguing detours, but we remained on the Espíritu Santo, now resembling a calm liquid swath through jungle. The forest is broken only by a new mangrove plantation (obligatorily planted by contractors who, in their zeal, had destroyed the former mangroves) and by the Río Grande Club de Pescadores (fishermen's club). Beyond the club, boats passed more often. Older drivers slowed down so their wakes would not rock our craft; youthful boaters seemed unaware of the problem.

The river makes one final loop, then empties into the sea. Visitors lounged on a semi-circular, palm-topped, white sand beach to one side of the mouth. We continued to a beach farther from the river where isolated palms, Australian pines and seagrapes provide limited shade. To the west the shoreline recedes and protrudes in giant arcs.

The ocean, shallow and warm, had a mucky bottom. Its water glistened, the hot land quivered, and clouds hung only above the ever-present Sierra de Luquillo. Pelicans perched on a branch in the water, while gulls remained in flight.

Disembarkation

At the end of the trip we spoke with Juan García, owner of La Viticuev, who wore a captain's cap and resembles a tanned and fit Bert Parks. From him, we learned the ocean flows into the river at high tide, carrying a variety of ocean fish — red snapper, sea bass, grouper, even sharks — in the heavier salt water underneath the fresh water. Although parts of the river are less than five feet deep, García claimed a 50-foot depth at the largest bend, Curva del Diablo (devil's curve).

But as we pulled and feathered paddles on the final upriver meander, we were moved by the placid well-being of the scene. The canoe skimmed along the lengthening mangrove shadows. The sun bowed out of the sky for the day. With the exception of birds scurrying for lodging and frogs and insects nervously announcing nightfall, the river seemed to have slipped into slow motion. In spite of sore muscles and reddened faces, we still felt that the canoe, slicing silently through the water, was the best way to discover the Espíritu Santo.

1990s UPDATE: La Lancha Paseadora closed several years ago. The river remains popular with canoeists and, more recently, kayakers, who take their own vessels. For those who would rather watch the river, there is a fishermen's co-op restaurant off Road 187 halfway between Highway 3 and the ocean. The small intake dam we encountered remains, but the original plans for a larger dam along the river have been shelved. For a glimpse of the upper Espíritu Santo, take Road 186 south into the mountains to Km. 22.8 and 18.4; the Sonadora, a tributary, is at Km. 19.5 These spots become crowded on weekends; paths paralleling the rivers lead to more isolated pools.

Mangrove-fringed estuary, lower Espíritu Santo (photo by Hugh Thorne)

THE LONG AND WINDING
TRAILS OF EL YUNQUE

Most visitors to the Caribbean National Forest, commonly known as El Yunque, park their cars at La Coca Falls and the observation tower, snap a few pictures and leave feeling content they have seen the rain forest. Though these stops are impressive, they merely scratch the surface of this 28,000-acre forest, the only area in Puerto Rico administered by the U.S. Forest Service and the only tropical forest in the federal system. For those interested in a more serious immersion, there are dozens of marked and well-maintained main trails and nameless and overgrown branch trails that wind through the exotic flora of the Sierra de Luquillo. El Toro Trail, Puerto Rico's longest maintained trail and its only one in the U.S. National Recreation Trail System, offers the best introduction to the forest's depths.

The opening frame

Travelers stop at a bend in the path. One grabs a vine to keep from slipping on the mossy stones. Around them, palms cling to mountain slopes. Overhead, a parrot squawks its rare presence, but the travelers do not notice. Their eyes focus on miles of wet jungle and a humpbacked peak far in the distance.

"Is that..."

"No. It's too far away."

The leader slowly nods. "That's it. El Toro peak."

Moans and invectives disturb the cool misty air. Then the travelers trudge onward.

Some background

El Toro Trail, also known (to a few) as the Tradewinds Trail, connects Road 191 in El Yunque with Road 186 in El Verde, eight miles away. On its way, it passes through four kinds of forest along a ridge of the Sierra de Luquillo, occasionally opening onto views as far west as San Juan, and east to the island of Vieques.

Members of the Civilian Conservation Corps (CCC) built the trail in the late 1930's to enable residents of the community of Cubuy to travel to the National Forest to work. Less than ten years later the CCC left, and the trail started to deteriorate. Heavy rainfall, hurricanes and landslides speeded up the deterioration in spite of periodic maintenance. Trail maintenance is an expensive, time-consuming task, especially in a rain

View toward Mount Britton, Caribbean National Forest

forest. Drainage ditches must be dug, gravel spread to prevent erosion, and landslides shored up — all this while preserving the natural forest beauty.

When the Forest Service decided to repair the trail again several summers ago, 60 youths from the Young Adult Conservation Corps worked almost three months before funding expired. One-third of the trail was neatly repaired; the remaining two-thirds of this ruggedly beautiful route is strewn with slippery rocks and mud.

Four forest types

Along the way the untutored eye notices a variety of vegetation that changes as deftly as a chameleon. Yet foresters know there is a pattern to this diversity, a predominance of certain tree species at different levels of altitude and rainfall.

The **tabonuco** forest type, which is the true rain forest vegetation, grows in elevations below 2,000 feet, where El Toro trail meets El Verde road. The deep soil, low altitude and moderately high rainfall here produce the greatest diversity of plants in the forest. Of 163 tree species in this area, the **tabonuco** is the most common. Its dark foliage, majestic height and occasional buttresses resembling elephants' feet make it one of Puerto Rico's most distinctive trees. When stained and finished, the wood resembles blond mahogany and has been used as an economical substitute.

In the higher elevations the swamp cyrilla **(palo colorado)** predominates over the other 52 tree species. Narrow leaves that turn red before falling cluster at the broom-shaped crown of this gnarled tree. Lianas dangle from its branches. Bromeliads growing on its limbs trap drinking water for tiny **coquí** frogs. Puerto Rican parrots, once nearly extinct, now — with much scientific help — slowly building up their population, nest in this area and on rare occasions are spotted from the trail.

Sierra palm forests proliferate in patches along steep slopes and gullies where little else will grow. The palm's smooth trunk, plumed fronds, white flower spikes and erect prop roots make it one of the easiest trees to identify.

On the highest peaks and ridges, where rain exceeds 150 inches yearly and winds wrack vegetation, the dwarf forest clings to a thin layer of soil. All trees here are stunted, twisted, draped with moss and wet with moisture. None grows above 20 feet. When the fogs roll in, effacing all but the nearest trees, one almost expects these elfin figures to flick their mossy cloaks and join their gnarled arms in an eerie, slow-motion dance.

Four hiking phases

Our hike was divided into four phases, which progressed from leisurely to diligent to dogged to rote.

During the leisurely phase the level trail, topped with gravel, enabled us to observe surrounding details. We counted three shelters and two camping tents. A saucer-shaped ledge seemed to have descended once upon a time from another world. Damp, shadowy forests of sierra palms, parasol tree ferns and bromeliads sprouting red blossoms contrast with sunny patches of grass and **palo colorados** dangling dry moss. We commented on a small washout, a woodpecker, a spider's web in a rotted log, a ribbon marking future repairs, a green lizard on moss, an absence of mosquitos. Streams falling over boulders enticed us to stop for drinks. Then we realized we had a long way to go.

In the diligent phase the rock trail commanded more attention than the lush ravines we were skirting. One member of the expedition prodded us onward with tunes from the French Foreign Legion. We debated unanswerable questions, such as which sex has more stamina. As silences grew, so did the imagination: we were soldiers in Southeast Asia searching for the runaway Cacciato; we were explorers about to discover a lost civilization; we were hobbits in an enchanted forest. Our pace quickened: El Toro had to be close, perhaps just around the bend...

Then we saw it, miles in the distance, and commenced the dogged phase of hiking, when intellect retreats and instinct assumes control. Attention focused on footsteps following the twisted path. Awesome views to the east coast and to the San José lagoon in San Juan went scarcely noticed. The trail becomes steeper and muddier, the forest shrinks to dwarf vegetation. We rounded one more bend and gained the summit of El Toro peak, highest point in the Sierra de Luquillo at 3,532 feet — five miles and three and a half hours after leaving our car.

The peak is topped with several boulders and a collapsed shelter. On clear days the view extends to San Juan, farmland around Humacao, Roosevelt Roads and Vieques. Visitors survey the miles of unbroken forest under which they have just hiked. When the fog creeps in, the view vanishes. Natural steps descend from the peak toward El Verde road, an hour's hike away. As our car was in El Yunque, we had to retrace our steps in what became the rote phase of the journey.

Sabana

In a search for information about the trail, Jerry Bauer — a forester in the Caribbean National Forest, known for his friendliness and his tobacco chewing — drove with me to the community of Sabana. Its 2,000 residents and high number of churches and bars are nestled in dense vegetation at the edge of the forest. Sabana is a town in miniature, with the usual proportion of elegant concrete residences, wooden homes and zinc-roofed shacks. At 7:30 in the evening, the area was darker than San Juan at any hour, and **coquí** frogs sounded as if in the thick of a revolution.

We were looking for Angelito Torres, and stopped at his small pastel house on stilts. Torres, who recently retired at the age of 75, had worked in the forest most of his life — in tree planting, nursery managing, forest improvement and inventory — and probably knows more about El Yunque than any living person. He went to school for one day, refusing to return because he was not taught anything he needed to know. Now Ph.D. botanists come to him when stumped about certain tree species.

Unfortunately, at that hour Torres was already asleep, his windows bolted. Yet across the street, behind a legume known as the poor man's orchid tree, was the bar of Manuel Vázquez who, with Torres, had worked on El Toro Trail in the days of the CCC. Vázquez grew up across the mountains in the town of Naguabo and began work in the forest as a laborer. Eventually he settled in Sabana and bought the bar, though he also continued to work in El Yunque. After speaking briefly about the trail, he invited us to a drink.

Inside the bar a pleasant woman introduced herself as Vázquez' wife. She soon led us back in time to the 1940's, when Sabana had no paved streets. Residents took off their shoes, waded through mud to their houses, then cleaned their feet in buckets of water. Houses were huts with straw roofs, dirt floors and **yagua** (sierra palm leaf) walls. Leaves were sewn together with needles of **ausubo** wood and thread from the fibrous **emajagua** bark. There was no electricity. Oil lamps left a sooty film on faces, and ashes from cooking fires were scattered by cats seeking warmth during the night.

In those days men earned a dollar for a long day's work and laborers made only $15 monthly. Often the pay came as chits to take to the general store and exchange for supplies. Shy **jíbaro** farmers hid in the woods when strangers passed, one of the many aspects of the 40's Mrs. Vázquez felt were no longer true.

Yes, she nodded, there had been undreamed of progress, much of which she attributed to former Gov. Muñoz Marín's vision. And yet — here she was not so sure — perhaps too much progress, for young men did not appreciate the marked increase in wages and young women preferred buying canned food to preparing their own fresh roots and plantains.

I sipped my drink and studied the formica bar, a dangling bulb, religious pictures, a juke box and a pool table surrounded by several young men. Outside, cool black air surrounded the orchid tree and the **coquís** chirped in revolt against the blasting **salsa** music.

"Progress," I mused, and returned to my drink.

Before we leave the forest, a glimpse of a branch trail

Progress had not reached the branch trail I visited half a year later. It is one of many small trails available to but rarely used by the public. Planned by the CCC for pedestrian use, this trail was only partially finished when World War II put an end to its construction. It looks like a copper-colored ribbon winding through the forest near El Toro Trail. At first it is easy to follow, though cluttered with rocks, logs, ferns and rivulets. One thick **palo colorado** tree along the path is estimated by some to be 1,500 years old. Other **palo colorados,** not so lucky, were cut for charcoal years ago and carried out on paths now obliterated.

The trail begins to deteriorate in an area full of tree buttresses, razor grass and branchlike vines which encircle trees. What looked like an abandoned prospecting site at the bank of a stream is actually a Forest

Sierra palm symmetry

Service project to study the ecology of the sierra palm forest. A patch of quartz sand nearby resembled butter pecan ice cream. Even stranger was a sandy, palm-lined section of another stream, a scene more reminiscent of the seashore than a rain forest. At certain times of the year the ground here is covered with crabs dining on palm fruit.

Soon afterward the trail narrows and becomes (if possible) more overgrown. We lost it once, backtracked, found it, lost it crossing a stream, found it, then lost it entirely.

"Around here is where the CCC stopped work", our guide admitted. "We'll have to go through forest until we get to the river."

Vines and roots tangle on the forest floor. When covered with leaves they form a springy path; when bare, they twist ankles. Had we not been with someone who knew the forest well, we most likely would have gotten lost at this point.

Along the way we entered a veritable field of bromeliads. A myriad of these bouquets of green arcs and red blossoms grew on branches, vines and ground. Other vegetation seemed a mere backdrop. Farther along, ribbons tied to trunks lead scientists through the forest. Occasionally birds nibble away these markers, leaving the scientists no better off than Hansel and Gretel.

We headed for the river, where water splashed over a series of boulders, in hopes that rock-hopping would prove easier than bushwhacking through well-woven underbrush. It did not, for the rocks were slippery from rain that had been falling intermittently all day. When a narrow path appeared parallel to the river, we gladly switched onto it.

The path passes an abandoned campsite, a concrete dam and several natural pools — secluded swimming holes — before it terminates at an overgrown road. The road enters an awesome hibiscus tunnel, then it too stops. We were once again in forest, stately **tabonuco** forest. Here there are taller trees, fewer exposed roots and less underbrush, and the air smells of leaves, not earth. With relative ease we reached the El Verde road, five miles and nine hours from our start.

1990s UPDATE: In September, 1989, Hurricane Hugo passed directly over El Yunque. Since then, the forest has recovered remarkably well. The foresters' Catalina Field Office (887-2875), (open weekdays only) is at the intersection of Road 191 and Road 988 to Sabana. Nearby a multi-million dollar center known as El Portal is scheduled to open in early 1996. (The Vázquez bar in Sabana closed several years ago.) El Toro Trail begins beyond the recreational area, shortly beyond the gate which marks the close of Road 191 due to a 20-year-old landslide farther down the road; it ends at Road 186 (approximately Km. 10.6). Hikers interested in branch trails should obtain a topographical map (on the second floor of the Minillas south building in San Juan, 721-8787, or the field office), wear long pants and sturdy shoes, carry a compass and speak to a forester first. Camping is permitted with a permit from the field office or visitor center. Ask about the safest place to leave your car.

A. *Cabo San Juan light, Fajardo* B. *Sailboats, Fajardo marina*

FAJARDO AND THE WORLD
OF SAILING

"Hoist the sail!"

The 27-foot boat headed into the wind. Its mainsail was cranked to the top of the mast. Lines at the stern slipped through the blocks. Rope flapped, sails fluttered. Suddenly, breathtakingly, the wind caught the sails and the engines sputtered out. The mainsail and jib lost their flutter and became taut white curves against the sky. Three and a half tons of teak-trimmed fiberglass tipped and glided through the sea.

I was about to explore the world of sailing off Fajardo, perhaps the best place in Puerto Rico to experience this world. Once a fishing village on the eastern tip of the island, Fajardo is now the home of several large marinas and a second home for thousands of boating enthusiasts.

Background

The reason for Fajardo's popularity is found in the sea and surrounding islands. The sea is clear and relatively calm. It is protected by a reef which extends from Cabezas de San Juan, the clawed peninsula forming Puerto Rico's northeast corner, to Culebra and beyond. Dozens of islands and cays, some secluded, some extremely popular, poke up out of the reef. Several (Los Farallones, Diablos) are little more than rocky peaks in the sea, while others (Cayo Icacos, Cayo Lobos) have beaches, shrub vegetation, palm trees and surrounding coral gardens. Intriguing names identify the islands, names like Isla de Aves (bird island), Isla Palominos (was this island once teeming with doves — **palominos**?), Isla de Ramos (who was Ramos?). All of them are within a two-hour sail from Fajardo. Many sailors here feel these islands compare favorably with their more famous Virgin Islands counterparts to the east.

Land attractions

Not all beauty of this pincer-shaped corner of Puerto Rico is on the ocean. Puerto Real, the dock area of Fajardo, has several points of interest. The pink stucco U.S. Customs House is the first stop for international sailors entering Puerto Rico. Large ferries run daily to the islands of Vieques and Culebra. A rusty furnace near the dock was once part of a lime mill; the lime was extracted from Cayo Icacos before the cay became government property. Small ferries leave the port regularly for Isleta Marina, a development of two condominiums, one boat yard and several docks on tiny Cayo Zancudo. Next to the Río Fajardo, a block from the docks, is Rosa's Restaurant, where the sailors I accompanied often went for seafood dishes and **arepas,** a slightly sweet fried puffy bread.

The drive along the coast toward the northeastern tip of the island passes Villa Marina and Puerto Chico Marina. Both are crammed with row after row of dazzling white boats: motorboats, launches, schooners, catamarans, yachts, motorsailors, boats for fishing, racing, diving, even a rowboat or two. Masts, stays and antennas angle into the sky.

This is Playa Sardinera, where numerous seafood restaurants face a beach cluttered with boats, drying nets and assorted flotsam. Beyond the beach an expanse of golf course to the right is part of El Conquistador, once an elegant hotel, now the property of the Transcendental Meditation Program.

The main road returns to the sea at Playa Soroco, more commonly known as the Seven Seas beach, a public bathing area and campsite for trailers. Palms line the white sand which curves for a mile in both directions. To the west a dirt road approaches Laguna Aguas Prietas and the beautiful, secluded Playa Convento. To the east a lagoon-fringed peninsula, Cabezas de San Juan, is topped by a neo-classical lighthouse. Plans to construct an exclusive development of homes with individual boat docks here were never approved, a result bemoaned by many businessmen but applauded by local fishermen and conservationists.

The road ends at Playa Las Croabas, where sailing sloops, boats made here in Puerto Rico, are moored in the bay. Several vendors were selling fish the day we visited.

Pushing off

For the novice, the world of sailing requires adjustments. It is different — from its vocabulary to its concerns. To sailors, ropes used in trimming sails are not ropes, but sheets. Toilets are heads. Left is port, but to move the boat to port you must push the rudder to starboard, or the right. Exciting bits of gossip are more commonly known as scuttlebutt. Landlubbers are told to be especially careful of the boom; they rub their heads painfully after discovering what it is.

Tacks and other sailing maneuvers have a sense of complicated urgency which is hard for the non-sailor to grasp, much less execute. (This newcomer regretted not having paid better attention to knots taught in scouting classes). Simple tasks like sitting and standing require special concentration on the rolling deck. Capricious winds are checked and charted and channeled into sails. Captains inevitably take on the aspect of Bligh in the eyes of enthusiastic but uncoordinated novices.

Sailing is also different in a much more beautiful sense. The beauty lies in the islands, the sea, the tranquillity.

A sampling of islands

Icacos is the most popular cay near Fajardo. Limegreen shrub covers most of it. Salt ponds, a tower and a ruin lie in its center. Posts in the sea are all that remain of an old dock. A thin strip of sand is available for sunning, clear water for swimming and clumps of coral for snorkeling.

The coral provides a magical kingdom of miniature towers and tunnels. Iridescent schools of fish swim around etched brain coral, fire-coral fingers and thimblelike clusters of soft coral. It is an ethereal kingdom, and vitally important as a protector of the shoreline. Unfortunately, this is not recognized by all boaters. Boat keels have leveled coral in shallow water. Anchors have ripped out coral lying in their paths. Visitors have broken off delicate, irreplaceable pieces for souvenirs. As more and more boats enter these waters, better education is needed.

Cayo Lobos (wolves cay) directly east of Icacos is a mysterious place. A dock stretches into pale water that was almost motionless the day we were there. Reef surrounds three sides of the small island. Nearby rocks partially eroded by the sea resemble giant toadstools. An abandoned hotel, complete with airstrip for small planes, was partly hidden behind palms and other vegetation. A family and entourage of dogs guarded the private property, but we were able to glimpse old volleyball courts, rooms with jalousie windows, and an assortment of bottles strung between branches. The hotel was closed some 15 years ago, apparently for want of business. According to local scuttlebutt, a lack of good docking facilities and a reputation as a place of wine, women and song aided in its decline. Joaquín A. Villamil, who once visited the hotel in a small boat wearing old clothes, carrying only fifty cents in his pocket and receiving some arched-eyebrow looks, now owns the cay.

Isla Palominos south of Lobos is also private. Its scrubby hill rises 165 feet out of the water, making it the highest island in the area. Visitors anchor offshore to swim and snorkel. To the southeast is Palominitos, a saucer-shaped speck of a sandbar, surrounded on three sides by shoals and topped in the center with a cropping of palms and seagrapes. Like Icacos, it is open to the public and ideal for swimming and snorkeling. On weekends, a semi-circle of anchored boats eclipses the sandbar.

The tranquillity of the sailing world is especially noticeable at night. We anchored in the protective leeward curve of one of the islands. Everyone was tired after the day at sea, and content with a very simple dinner. The water scarcely rippled. A gray sky silhouetted the darker island. The only noises came from halyards clanging on the mast, from the wind moaning through the rigging, from sailors conversing in a nearby yacht. Above, constellations spun their ageless myths to those who could read them. Far away, the lighthouse blinked its warning, and the lights of Fajardo shimmered and beckoned. We were not tempted by their beckoning at all, although a sailor later mentioned that when **he** sees those lights after a month at sea he is desperate to reach shore.

Ventures into the boating world for the boatless

Starting with the most economical, at 1992 prices $6 ($10 on weekends) will take you to Culebra or Vieques and back on the ferry. Several sloops in Las Crobas bay rent (with captain) for $60, and sail to the island of your fancy —within reason, of course. Guests — up to six — must supply their own lunches and snorkeling or fishing gear. The boast are simple, with open holds where passengers sit on benches. Jack Becker, a wiry sailor with white hair, beard and eyepatch, captains the best known charter. His 40-foot catamaran, the Spread Eagle, sails from Villa Marina on all-day trips, usually to Icacos and Palominitos. Captain Jack supplies snorkeling equipment and a buffet lunch, all for $45 per person.

Several of the big San Juan hotels offer all-day excursions to Fajardo that start in San Juan, and the marinas can direct visitors to boats for rent or charter. Costs for weekend trips on luxury yachts, with drinks, food and sports equipment included, can climb to more than $1,000.

1990s UPDATE: Road 195 connects Highway 3 with Puerto Real, Fajardo's port. Road 987 parallels the coast to Las Croabas bay. El Conquistador passed through its transcendental mediation phase and is now a world-class resort. Seven Seas is a public beach (see the Vieques article). Las Cabezas de San Juan has recently opened to the public as a lovely nature reserve with lagoons and mangrove forest, a century-old lighthouse and sweeping views. Guided tours of the site can be made through the Conservation Trust of Puerto Rico (722-5882); reservations are required. Also new is the elegant Puerto del Rey marina southeast of Fajardo proper. Largest marina in the Caribbean, Puerto del Rey (860-1000) is the likely place to find that weekend luxury yatch. Captain Jack now captains a smaller, motorized boat, but his Spread Eagle (863-1905) continues to ply the waters. Call 863-0852 for ferry schedules. For more information about hotels and water sports centers, see **Qué Pasa** or other local tourism magazines.

A. *Boys fishing from pier* B. *Cabo San Juan lighthouse seen from Seven Seas beach*

BIRD BANDING ON CULEBRA

Culebra, an island still little known for its pristine beaches, spectacular coral reefs and languorous tropical living, is even less known as the site of the Culebra National Wildlife Refuge, 23 offshore islands reserved for more than 10 marine bird nesting colonies including the largest sooty tern colony in Puerto Rico. One June weekend I flew over to band the terns with members of the U.S. Fish and Wildlife Service.

Transitions

Small planes regularly lift off from Isla Grande Airport on the short flight to Culebra. San Juan bay's brown water becomes a cloudy blue along the north coast. Beyond Fajardo, translucent sea exposes rims of underwater coral. Pilots aim for the pivot of a hilly, plier-shaped island. The planes sway onto a miniature runway next to Culebra's one-room terminal.

The sea change involves more than colors. It also seems to cushion Culebra against the bustle and sophistication of contemporary Puerto Rico. In the mysterious ways of small islands with few phones and seemingly fewer clocks, when I arrived in Culebra the bird-banding group was parked by chance in front of the Happy Landing Restaurant next to the airport, able to take me to their camp.

Attractions for humans

Culebra is a sun-bleached mound topped with dry scrub and coastal forests, cattle pastures and the mostly bright-colored homes for its 2,000 residents. In spite of the island's languorous pace, its location halfway between Puerto Rico and St. Thomas has resulted in several historical distinctions. Reportedly visited by Columbus on his second voyage in 1493, Culebra was inhabited first by Indians, then pirates, then Spanish settlers. Following the 1898 Spanish-American War, the U.S. Navy opened facilities on Culebra's public lands and remained there until 1975. Ensenada Honda, a 42-foot-deep, two-mile-long bay, was the Navy's principal anchorage area in the Caribbean before Guantánamo.

Culebra's numerous beaches, usually semi-deserted, attract today's visitors. Bone-white sand and clear water characterize all of them. Some

Sooty terns, Culebra National Wildlife Refuge

lie at the end of rough jeep roads. Many have colorful fish and coral communities (and a few unexploded projectiles) in their waters. One especially popular beach, Playa Flamenco, arcs for more than a mile between a mottled blue bay and low-lying forest with patches of Australian pine. Snorkeling and scuba diving are common on Culebra, as is boating — an easier way than driving to reach some beaches — and, of course, sunbathing.

Dewey, Culebra's sole town, is wedged between Ensenada Honda and the Caribbean. Its buildings, starkly bright under the intense sunlight, are very dark at night, when few lights counteract the blackness. One evening we zigzagged twice across the tiny town, taking several side streets (they all seem to be side streets, actually) before deciding to stop at El Navegante, one of Dewey's three restaurants. Here we ate fish and watched sailboat masts doodle against the dark sky.

Attractions for birds

While waves of Culebra settlers have come and gone, a steady group of sea birds has nested, roosted, fished and flown over the island. President Theodore Roosevelt recognized this (how he did remains a mystery, as no records have been saved) and in 1909 declared all public lands in Culebra, including offshore islands, a preserve for native birds. This refuge now consists of 23 offshore islands and four tracts of land on Culebra and is reserved for communities of red-billed tropicbirds (the only place in Puerto Rico they are found), brown boobies (one of only three major colonies in Puerto Rico) and 11 other marine bird species, including laughing gulls and sandwich terns. The most abundant sea birds in the refuge are the sooty terns **(booby).**

The objective of the U.S. Fish and Wildlife Service (FWS), which administers the refuge, is to maintain the diverse wildlife species and their natural habitat. For this reason only two of the refuge islands are open to the public, and stiff fines are imposed on those who "egg" (take eggs, often for folk remedies), trap or kill any native birds of Puerto Rico.

At the Department of Natural Resources headquarters at Lower Camp, Culebra's original settlement, we watched a swirling sunset and swatted prolific sandflies while FWS Refuge Manager Sean Furniss explained the purposes of the next day's bird banding. The banding, which requires permits from both Federal and Commonwealth governments, helps determine sooty tern migration routes (where do the birds go during the eight months they are not nesting?), colony site shifts (barring changes in habitat, birds unerringly return to the birth sites when nesting), and life spans.

In the gray dawn of the next day, having slept in a bunkhouse and showered in a horse tackle shed, the bird banding group listened to the matinal calls of roosters, pigeons, zenaida doves, green herons, yellow warblers and the "rat-rat-rat" of our motorboat warming up.

A. *Cayo Yerba* B. *Sooty terns in flight, Península Flamenco* C. *Sooty tern egg*

Cay-hopping

Coleridge's "the fair breeze blew, the white foam flew, the furrow followed free" came to mind as our Boston whaler motored past several flan-shaped cays toward Cayo del Agua, once heavily bombed by the Navy, now considered a likely location for tern nesting. As on most of the cays, boulders, grass, seagrapes, shrubs, dildo and turks-head cacti and white-blossomed **alelí**, closely related to frangipani trees, predominate. A search of this miniature island revealed Bahama duck eggs in a feather-lined nest, zenaida dove nestlings, a rusted projectile and target tires, but no sooty tern nests.

The boat then pointed toward hump-shaped, cliff-lined Cayo Yerba, one of the two refuge cays densely covered with sedge. There, darkening the bright blue sky, were thousands of hovering sooty terns. The bird banding was about to begin.

Terns posed and a brown noddy nested in the cay cliffs. Furniss set up equipment in a shaded cavity while the rest of us followed barely perceptible tern trails through the grass, stepping with care around eggs and nestlings. It was an eerie scene of waist-high sedge, tree skeletons, hobbling and swooping birds, and the din of protective chiding.

We grabbed the nest watchers, using sedge as a bind, snuggled them under our arms and brought them, squirming and pecking at wrists and finger webs, to Furniss, who clamped uniquely numbered aluminum bands on flailing legs and released the birds into the air. Every tenth bird was eased into a sack and placed on a dangling pesola scale to be weighed. Furniss also measured wing chord lengths, which he recorded in a green book. Regurgitated food — at times spewed down banders' pants — was scooped into glass vials for later analysis of the sooties' diet. In two hours we banded 141 birds, and later discovered that two birds had actually been banded the previous year on this same cay.

The next stop was Cayo Luis Peña, one of the two cays in the refuge open to the public, from sunrise to sunset, for recreational activities related to wildlife and wildlands. Although at one time two families of cattle ranchers settled on this 107-acre island, it is still covered with a large tract of remnant forest which includes a thin-stemmed endemic bamboo. Extensive grassbeds off its eastern shore once supported a large number of conch, now depleted by fishermen.

On the other side of a white beach, past boulders decked with sweet smelling **alelí**, were two nests containing white-tailed tropicbirds — down-coated birds with beaks and mascara-black eyes. After a non-ornithological swim in transparent water lined with coral, we returned to Lower Camp.

The other cay open to the public is Culebrita — hilly, scrub-forested, one mile long and pinched in the center. A large bay, a mangrove-lined lagoon, impeccable beaches and superb coral reefs distinguish the cay. A rectangular lighthouse on its southeastern extension is listed in the National Register of Historic Places. Two plants endemic to Culebrita **(Caesalpinia culibrae** and **Justicia culebritae)** have been proposed as additions to the Federal List of Endangered Species. Turtles and red-billed tropicbirds nest here. Bahama ducks (white-cheeked pintails) skim the brackish water of its lagoon.

Back on Culebra

Monte Resaca, a recent refuge acquisition, hosts an unusual boulder forest where **cupey** and fig trees, bromeliads, orchids, vine-like endemic **Peperonia wheeleri** (in danger of extinction), anthurium and vine cacti tangle on a rock-strewn hillside. This forest is the critical habitat for the Culebra giant anole lizard, officially last recorded in 1932, although reportedly sighted since then by knowledgeable island residents. Far below the forest is Playa Resaca, a secluded nesting place for half-ton leatherback turtles.

Meddlesome mosquitoes ensured that our visit was brief.

Peninsula Flamenco, the northwest extension of Culebra, resembled a setting for a Hitchcock nightmare or a Sinai spectacular the morning we drove there. Bald hills are spotted with mesquite, cacti and giant milkweed. Rusted tank carcasses, water-filled bomb craters and barbed wire — leftovers from former Navy gunnery and bombing practice — "relieve" the starkness. A jeep road leading to the peninsula is framed between "cool" sea and "hot" sky. A ghostly moon, an orange sun and thousands of terns flying in graceful chaos, yapping their agitation, garnished the cloudless sky. Bird banders wore helmets, caps (one advertising Dekalb Corn, another dubbing the wearer a Jack Daniels Field Tester), hats or bandanas to guard against the sunlight.

Peninsula Flamenco is a good example of a shifting colony site and the complex factors involved in wildlife habitats. Although the Navy's departure from Culebra in 1975 was a relief to most residents, it proved disastrous to the sooty terns on Flamenco. The bombing had produced a grassy habitat ideal for terns, and Navy fences protected the colonies. After the Navy left, cows were turned loose and ate the grass, and people "egged" the birds, reducing the colony to 20,000 in 1976. That year the tip of the peninsula was fenced, and personnel from the Culebra Conservation and Development Authority began a 24-hour watch during nesting season. Yet in 1980 there were no sooties nesting on Flamenco; its habitat may have become too overgrown. In 1981 they were back, possibly because someone had cut the fence and several cows straggled in, chomping the old grass, permitting new grass to shoot up. One can imagine the sooties sitting around their nests at night now, reminiscing about the good old days when there was bombing.

While we banded on Flamenco, the airborne terns would suddenly stop their haphazard hovering and swoop to one side in startling unison, apparently a sign of panic. (Due to a puzzling lack of waterproof plumage, these birds cannot land on water. They seem to be in almost constant motion for six or more non-breeding months, landing occasionally on flotsam, driftwood or offshore islands, possibly sleeping in flight.) In two and a half hours we banded 208 birds, one of which had been previously banded in 1966 in the Dry Tortugas by the Florida Audubon Society.

Afterward, we rewarded our efforts with a swim at Playa Flamenco, joining isolated clusters of bathers and picnickers who looked like Lilliputians dwarfed by the ample curve of beach. The water was clear, the sand bleached, the atmosphere tranquil. It was with much reluctance that we returned to Lower Camp and, for some, home to city life.

Noddy tern nesting, Cayo Yerba

1990s UPDATE: Small planes reach Puerto Rico's offshore islands (Culebra and Vieques) from Isla Grande and Fajardo, and ferries leave from Fajardo's port (see the Fajardo article). For information about accomodations, call the Culebra Bureau of Tourism (742-3291) or check **Qué Pasa** or other local tourism magazines. Hurricane Hugo churned over both islands in 1989, but most tourism establishments have been restored or replaced. Culebra remains refreshingly undeveloped, although a new paved road or two have opened up in the past years. The Happy Landing still greets airport arrivals, the Culebra giant anole remains elusive, and the terns are alive and well. From May to July beach patrols protect breeding leatherback turtles; contact the refuge (see below) if you want to help. Boats to visit reefs and offshore islands can be rented or chartered in Dewey through local boatowners.

A NOTE TO BIRD WATCHERS: If you want a closer look at the seabirds, or if you would like to help the scientists who study them, contact the Culebra Wildlife Refuge manager at Lower Camp (742-0115, 851-7258). A number of sites in Puerto Rico proper, including the Punta Santiago lagoons of Humacao and the Guánica and Maricao Forest Reserves, attract large numbers of migratory and resident birds. The Cabo Rojo Wildlife Refuge (851-7258), also run by U.S. Fish and Wildlife, can orient you to the birds of the southwest. **A Guide to the Birds of Puerto Rico and the Virgin Islands** by Herbert A. Raffaele remains invaluable for island bird watchers.

A. *Bicycling on Vieques* B. *Bicycles at rest*

VIEQUES BY BIKE

For the moment it seemed we were flying. Trees, homes, dogs and pastures whizzed by, while a white-winged dove kept pace. Far below, a palm-lined bay shimmered around moored boats. The wind caressed us as it parted; it was the only sound we heard. All was right with the world as our bicycles sped down a hill on the island of Vieques.

Crossing the channel

Friday, 8:15 a.m. "Bicycles are absolutely prohibited on the passenger launch." The notice seemed to glare from the Fajardo Ferry Terminal. It was not a propitious sign; it meant waiting two hours for the slower cargo ferry and remaining on Vieques until Monday instead of Saturday as we had planned. No amount of reasoning persuaded the man in charge. At 9:15 the half-filled launch pushed off without us. "That's a tough break," sympathized the bilingual soda vendor across the street.

At the Vieques Culebra en Fajardo Restaurant we had coffee. Our bicycles, which we had to leave outside, were encumbered with saddle and handlebar bags, a tire pump and water bottles. Although worried we would not have enough provisions for a three-day camping trip, we decided to continue.

The cargo ferry arrived late. Amid the squawking of horns and loudspeakers and the nauseous smell of diesel fuel, it was unloaded and reloaded. Trucks carrying gravel, cement blocks, reinforcement bars, concrete; an old turquoise Cadillac, a station wagon and several small cars; two bicycles and one lawnmower passed over the plank. The captain, with hair slicked back and wearing a white shirt, shouted directions while dangling a cigarette between missing teeth.

At last the ferry eased from the dock. During the hour-and-a-half ride, Puerto Rico blurred, contracted and disappeared, then Vieques appeared, expanded and came into focus.

Vieques ferry landing

Isabel Segunda

Isabel Segunda

A low lighthouse, pastel houses and semi-arid vegetation greet passengers on arriving in Isabel Segunda, the main town of Vieques. Inland, the usual municipal buildings, church and school surround a gold and white plaza with India-laurel fig trees. Streets southwest of the plaza are wide and tree lined; wooden residences outnumber stores. Streets to the northeast are cluttered with cars and dusty shops.

A narrow road weaves between homes to the town's fort, built in the mid-1800's during the reign of Isabel II of Spain. Brick arches lead to unfurnished rooms with wooden beams and open patios, and to a dark semi-circular chamber. Some of the wooden windows are shuttered; others open onto views of well-manicured grounds, the town, dry hills and glistening sea. Cannons pointing toward the bay apparently were never fired.

The fort guide, Gregorio Mercado Huerta, is a wrinkled man in a felt hat, whose thick glasses and two remaining teeth seem to accentuate his smiling eyes and mouth. He was adding numbers out loud as he sat on a bench under a legume tree but stopped to talk with us about the fort and life in Vieques.

When Mercado was 12, he worked 12 hours a day in sugar cane fields for 25 cents. A white flag raised on a hill signaled the end of the work day. He later became a carpenter, aiding in the fort's restoration. According to Mercado, the years before the end of sugar cane harvesting in 1943 were ones of misery and poverty. Though there are still few jobs, he feels the U.S. has helped the island, and life now is ten times better than in his youth. Six of his seven children live in the States. He interspersed his musings with chuckles and jokes. We departed with much waving and well wishing.

Several restaurants in Isabel Segunda offer simple meals. We sampled tasty fried parrotfish and **arepas** (puffed bread) at Ocean View Restaurant, beef stew at Boricua Bar, a tortilla at El Yate and coffee at Starboard Light Café. The café is a picturesque whitewashed building with wood trim, a starboard light and an anchor.

The café's owner, a white-haired World War II Navy veteran who still wears a crewcut, had been stationed in Vieques and decided to resettle here. He insisted we serve ourselves coffee as he nursed a hangover. A well-dressed Viequense also entered for coffee. A woman stopped to smoke a cigarette and chat. A man who seemed to be gay sat at one of the tables. All mingled amiably in the café.

Bicycling

"Bicycling is the most efficient means of transportation," bike enthusiasts maintain. Perhaps — although the belief will seem somewhat naive when cyclists sweat and strain and scarcely progress up steep stretches of back roads on Vieques. However, once the cyclist whirs along the top of this 1,000-foot-high island, it does seem the ideal way to observe the countryside. Elegant homes with sloping roofs and wide verandahs face postcard views of the town of Esperanza, Sun Bay and the Caribbean. Small settlements nestle in cropped hills resembling Western ranch land. Bright flowers contrast with deep green forest vegetation. Yet the views blur on the downhill stretch when the vehicles, moving at breakneck speed, demand attention.

Cycling has its drawbacks. Vieques' main roads, though exceptionally smooth, are hilly, narrow and congested near town, and drivers are not accustomed to watching for bicycles. Biking is not yet widely accepted as a sport in Puerto Rico; the reception given riders at times resembles that once given to hippies. Sudden downpours, common in the tropics, can reduce clothes and gear to sodden lumps and, as happened to me, can turn carefully detailed notes into Rorschach blots. Yet this mode of transportation **is** efficient, as well as economical and healthy. With our bicycles we were able to lunch in Esperanza, snorkel at a beach with fish and soft coral near the airport, dine three miles away at Isabel Segunda, then recross the island for a nightcap at La Casa del Francés Guesthouse. All this was done without expensive stops at gas stations, and with the added bonuses of unobstructed views, unpolluted air and motorless sounds.

Camping

Bright streetlamps line the road to Sun Bay (also spelled Sombé), site of a public beach and campground. The night guard was cautious until we produced our camping permits; then he became garrulous as he showed us several choice sites near the lights and cautioned against delinquents who have been known to raid the area when visitors are not around. He oriented us further, pointing out clean restrooms, water faucets and showers available during the day for a dime.

The beach at night is lovely. Gray water laps a bay shaped like a half sun. Salt-scented breezes and charcoal silhouettes of palms and seagrapes add to the serene atmosphere, marred only by a myriad of biting **mimis.** Two other camping groups were bedded down in tents. We had brought no tent. Although this seemed a good decision as we fell asleep under a canopy of dark sky and occasional shooting stars, we came to rue such a lack of foresight: twice that night it rained.

In the morning we dried out on a long walk along the beach. Its expansive curve leads to an old dock near the town of Esperanza to the west and several smaller bays to the east. Mounds of dried seaweed, coconut husks and tiny seashells line the sand. The first bay to the east, reached from the beach by a jeep road bordered by dusty legume vegetation wrapped in vines and cacti, is the small, almost perfectly rounded Bahía Media Luna. Butterflies flit through the branches of numerous seagrape trees which surround its turquoise water. Unfortunately, litter detracts from the delightful setting.

Searching for beaches

"Can we bribe you with fried chicken and a bit of wine?" asked the husband of a couple who invited us to join them in a drive to Blue Beach.

The Navy guard smiled and shook his head. "Come back soon," he urged. "When there are no maneuvers, these roads and beaches are open to the public."

The maneuvers which thwarted our entry onto Navy land were part of Ocean Venture, a major multi-nation Naval exercise conducted every August on Vieques. Blue Beach (also called Bahía Tapón) is said to have the best snorkeling on the island, although the entire southeast coast is scalloped with small bays and deserted beaches, many with coral reefs. There are also several forested areas, lagoons, turtle nesting habitats and archaeological sites within the Navy's boundaries. Mangroves in Punta Arenas on the northwest coast — nesting and breeding site for endangered white-crowned pigeons, herons and egrets — are off limits to the public for ecological reasons.

In part because of maneuvers, the Sun Bay and Bahía Media Luna beaches, not on Navy land, were crowded with people and cars. The small, box-shaped Bahía Novillo beach to the east of Media Luna had a more intimate feel. Seagrapes provided shade for picnic lunching here. Local fishermen followed a path across coral rock to a wide bay called Puerto Mosquito. Eager to snorkel, we swam across this bay to what turned out to be a reef of leveled elkhorn coral, apparently destroyed by a hurricane.

Later, we drove past horses grazing along a dirt back road as we neared the edge of doorknob-shaped Puerto Mosquito. The area has a strange, abandoned quality. A lagoon encircles dozens of drowned trees and palms, and old cars and appliances rust along the road. Around the bay, late afternoon sun lit dun-colored tidal flats and a fringe of mangroves; the flats and the mangroves stimulate the water's rare and fragile phosphorescence. It is best viewed by boat on a moonless night when the billions of microscopic organisms shine brightly.

La Casa del Francés

A dirt driveway curves to a sprawling white house, partly hidden by trees and bushes and distinguished by shutter windows and a gable roof. Steps ascend to the black and white tile floors of a wide verandah which encircles much of the house. Inside, a two-story atrium and high ceiling fans grace rooms leading to an open dining area which faces a pool and a profusion of flowering plants. A woman with a parasol and billowy dress would not seem out of place here.

A. *Portion of Sun Bay* B. *Diving fun*

The house was built in the early 1900's by a French sugar plantation owner, apparently for his fiancée, but she was not impressed and returned to France within a year. A strike at the Esperanza mill prompted the Frenchman to sell his plantation in 1915, yet the house is still known as La Casa del Francés.

A patio bar shaded by a lacy network of leaves and branches provides a meeting place for guests and residents. One Viequense recently arrived from Boston broached the controversy of the Navy's presence on Vieques, the only time it was brought up during our stay. During World War II, the Navy acquired title to some 70% of the island, over half of which is now being leased to the Vieques Cattlemen's Association. Arguments over who really controls the Vieques economy and how much damage Naval bombing practice on Punta Este actually does to the island's resources can erupt into a Pandora's box of complexities and emotional partisanship. Perhaps for that reason the topic is rarely mentioned with visitors (and not detailed further here).

Esperanza

Esperanza, remnant of the sugar cane era, is now home to many of the island's fishermen and to a new island **parador**, Villa Esperanza. A skeletal dock and rusting sugar boilers lie "in state" next to ketches, sloops, dories and motorboats in the bay. El Quenepo Restaurant, where we sampled conch turnovers called **pastelillos**, is shaded by a tree of the same name. A woman relaxing on a hammock next to the tackle and gear lockers of the Vieques Fishermen's Association building seemed oblivious to the pellucid bay and dry nubby hills in the distance.

The Cerromar Restaurant a mile west of Esperanza is decorated with nets, shells, plants and a sea mural. Here we had a delicious meal that included grouper, barbecued ribs and breadfruit fritters. The only difficulty was having to bicycle back to Esperanza coddling heavy stomachs.

On the way we passed Duffy's, a guesthouse with a front porch bar/restaurant crowded with Saturday night revelers. Amber lights formed a background for laughter, loud voices and clinking glasses. It was as if Duffy's were rebelling, shaking its fist at the vast darkness of the sea.

***

Passengers stood on the Isabel Segunda dock waiting for the ferry to return them to Fajardo. The boat arrived, unloaded, loaded and edged away from the dock, the buoys and finally the bay. We noticed the lighthouse, the homes, the fort. Soon these faded, and we noticed the long, low strip of semi-arid island extending east and west. Soon even that faded, and we contented ourselves with the sea.

1990s UPDATE: Bicycles are still allowed only on the cargo ferries (863-0852) from Fajardo. In part because of Hurricane Hugo several of the restaurants mentioned in the article have closed or changed names, and others have opened. Villa Esperanza (742-8675) lost its trademark warehouse to Hugo and is currently not a Tourism-sponsored **parador**; Casa del Francés (741-3751) endures. The fort at Isabela Segunda has been restored and is open weekends, and a sea promenade has been inaugurated in Esperanza. I eventually visited the Navy beaches, which were worth the wait; an especially nice ride is to Green Beach on the northeast coast, past an unfinished pier stretching toward Puerto Rico. Car rentals and reservations to visit Puerto Mosquito can be made at hotels. For more information see the Culebra article or contact Vieques Tourism (741-4752).

Punta Mula lighthouse, Isabel Segunda

A NOTE ON CAMPING: To camp on Sun Bay, you must obtain a permit from the Department of Recreation and Sports (724-2500), which also offers camping at several other public beaches, including Seven Seas in Fajardo, Añasco, Luquillo and Punta Guilarte in Arroyo. The Department of Natural Resources offers camping in several of its mountain and karst forests and on Mona Island (see the Karst Country and Mona articles), and the Caribbean National Forest also permits camping (see the Yunque article). There are a few privately run, crowded-on-weekends campsites; try locating them through the **alcaldías** (town halls). Due to the island's high rainfall, abundant bugs and large population, camping is not a common pastime, and camping in isolated, unsupervised areas is not recommended.

A ROUTE OF MANY FACETS —
SOUTHEAST PUERTO RICO

Imagine this fantasy: You fish in a blue mountain lake where bass leap above the water and forests line its banks. You get into your car and two hours later are tanning on a wide white sand beach surrounded by Indian almonds, seagrapes, coconut palms — and a century-old lighthouse. You drive another hour, stopping in time to rush for shelter from an afternoon downpour under an elephantine **yautía** leaf in the center of rain forest vegetation.

Fantastic though it may seem, this close proximity of mountain lake, rain forest and tropical beach does exist. The lake and forest — both called Carite — are part of the mountainous Sierra de Cayey which slopes toward the hilly Cuchilla de Pandura range which tumbles onto the beaches and clear waters of southeast Puerto Rico. Not only are these sites within a two-hour drive from San Juan, they are also connected by roads that form part of the island's Ruta Panorámica, looping past scenes of exhilarating diversity in one of the most pleasant day trips on the island.

Yabucoa

The southeast circuit starts in Yabucoa, a municipality of some 30,000 residents nestled between sugar cane fields and hills. Although there are roads skirting the downtown area, we decided to drive into its center, past the usual stores selling furniture, clothes and shoes, banks, pharmacies and a marketplace brimming with plantains and various roots. We regretted our choice of routes when we became stalled in a massive traffic jam. The sun beat down relentlessly, and a cacophony of loudspeakers around us blared **salsa** music, the day's bargains and political ditties.

Small **público** buses lined an entire side of the town plaza. A modern concrete Catholic church fills most of the plaza itself, replacing a smaller church once located on the same site. Blue stained glass sparkles above louvered windows. Although this lack of open space in a plaza is not customary, the arrangement must please Yabucoa's religious leaders, for the townspeople now mingle on the steps of the church.

Once an important center for the sugar industry, Yabucoa is still tied economically to the Roig sugar mill north of town. In addition, several companies, including Sun Oil and Union Carbide, have factories on the

A. *View toward Vieques, Punta Yeguas* B. *Nuestra Madre shrine, Carite Forest* C. *Charco Azul, Carite For*

outskirts of town. East of Yabucoa a large scooped out harbor, deep enough for oil tankers to enter, marks the port zone, inactive the Saturday we visited it. A dredging bucket was rusting in the salty air, and discarded white metal contraptions, mottled with barnacles, looked like industrial dinosaurs. A fishnet partly covered one of these. Two men carried poles and tackle to the edge of the dock. Pelicans seemed to follow invisible rollercoaster tracks above the water. A tugboat waited for Monday.

To the lighthouse

After Yabucoa, we followed the Ruta Panorámica in a 25-mile clockwise circle around the 1,700-foot-high Cerro Santa Elena. Our first stop was Balneario Lucía, a ghost bathing resort with neglected restaurants. A dense plantation of coconut palms covers most of the grounds. The seedlings were planted in symmetrical rows, but the trunks grew in all directions, creating a look of abandoned neatness. Metal bands on the trunks keep rats from climbing. According to people who vow having seen it happen, when there are no such bands, rats with a penchant for primitive piloting climb the trunks, nibble a hole in the coconuts, lap out the milk, crawl through the hole into the nut, gnaw off the stem and sit inside the shell as it makes its breakneck descent to the ground. (I have not been able to verify this curious practice.)

After Lucía, the road curves around Punta Yeguas. At each ascending loop, there is a more spectacular view of parched grazing hills and nubby trees descending to a V-shaped point. The sea is mottled turquoise and navy. Vieques is a hazy bulge on the horizon. El Horizonte Restaurant was built on the pinnacle of this view. The bi-level restaurant, decorated in harmonizing natural woods, offers local dishes, fresh seafood and live music on weekends.

The road continues past cows, stick and barbed-wire fences and dry vegetation toward Punta Tuna, where the hills extend into the sea. A lighthouse perched on this point next to a small, secluded beach marks the official junction of the east and south coasts.

Built in the 1890 s, the lighthouse is part of a unified system of some dozen lighthouses planned and constructed by the Spanish colonial government to protect imports and exports by lighting up Puerto Rico for traders. The design of the system (plagued with the usual budgetary problems) was organized down to the size and number of rooms in each lighthouse, rules for maintenance (how to remove dirt from the rotating devices, how to polish the optics) and dress codes (crude drill uniforms with white buttons inside the lighthouse, blue drill with gold buttons outside).

Punta Tuna Light Station, a white rectangular base topped with a black tower containing a lantern and a black weathervane, is now run by the U.S. Coast Guard. It is the only station in Puerto Rico still manned.

A. *Balneario Lucía* B. *Lago Carite* C. *Punta Tuna lighthouse*

On to Maunabo

Playa Maunabo on the other side of the lighthouse was our beach "find" of the day. As the road lowers to the coast, we saw a wide strip of sand stretching almost a mile to the next range of hills that slope to the sea. The sand glistens with gray specks, volcanic in origin. Beach trees cluster around a dilapidated picket fence. Thatched **bohío** shelters provide additional shade.

Drinks and snacks are sold in a large shanty (lacking bathrooms) which is frequented by local residents, overwhelmingly men. We ordered salty fish soup and freshly made conch salad, both served in plastic cups, then sat at a table to watch the beach activities.

A group of local boys was playing baseball: the bat was a length of bamboo, the bases were coconut husks and a peeling rowboat served as backstop. The teams were organized in a haphazard manner, with a half dozen shortstops, but no one seemed concerned. A short, skinny boy belted a triple, and the biggest player barely tipped the ball; voices scoffed with good-humored enthusiasm.

After lunch we walked on the straight, level beach. The short, skinny boy slammed a homerun when we returned. We slipped into the water and relaxed on the sand; the teams swelled and shrunk but did not disband. When the sun began to sear us, we looked up at the cool mountains. It was time to explore them. We left, with the game still in progress.

The Ruta Panorámica twists through the outskirts of Maunabo, built in a valley between two mountain ranges. Cane fields surround sun-lightened houses and several steeples in this town, a third the size of Yabucoa.

Transitional roads

Beyond Maunabo to the top of the Cuchilla de Pandura mountains the vegetation is a deeper green and slick with moisture. Volcanic boulders as large as the area's colorful homes poke through woods full of breadfruit, coffee and **quenepa** trees (which bear small, edible fruit). Steep paths connect the homes. Bars built on the shoulder of the road face views of the mountains dropping into the Yabucoa valley which rises into a more massive, distant mountain range: the Sierra de Cayey.

Sloping patches of **yautía, ñame** and plantains — staples of the rural diet — replace level sugar cane fields as the road, actually a mere country lane, rises into the mountains. Soon even these patches of cultivation are replaced by dense forest the color of malachite, the texture of cobwebs. This is the Carite Forest Reserve.

The Carite (Guavate) Forest Reserve

The reserve's location off the Ponce Expressway near Cayey makes it the most accessible of Puerto Rico's own upland forest reserves to residents and visitors in San Juan (El Yunque, equally accessible, is federally run). Its more than 6,000 acres were originally purchased for watershed protection and forestry. Native trees (of which the sierra palms are most obvious) mingle with imported varieties including teak and mahogany. Through several gaps in the vegetation visitors view the south coast.

We entered the forest from the east. Wet tangles of vegetation were occasionally broken by landslides spilling from steep clayey shoulders onto the recently built road. Heavy rainfall and clay soils make this area prone to slides. At the top of one of the forest's peaks, patches of dwarf forest — not as bent and soggy as in El Yunque but wondrous nonetheless — surround a communication tower. The low, crooked vegetation is caused by high humidity in the air and soil: tree roots have difficulty getting oxygen from the sodden soil, and transpiration (sweating) into the wet air is also difficult; both are essential for normal growth. Construction of communication towers, nemeses of most island peaks, has reduced this rare forest by nearly 20 percent in Carite.

Cerro La Santa, highest peak in Carite at 3,000 feet, was named for a kindly woman who lived here during Spanish colonial times. Nuestra Madre, a Catholic spiritual meditation center on another peak, permits visitors to stroll through its grounds. During the Easter season, thousands pilgrimage to this site, where many believe the Virgin Mary appeared. In contrast, the reserve also contains the Guavate Penal Camp. Low drab buildings surround a field where men were playing baseball or watching from the stands. The camp is minimum security; some inmates even help with reforestation projects. The objectives of the Forest Service's reforestation program are to enrich poor forests, reforest bare areas to prevent erosion and produce wood for commercial use.

At the ranger station we met members of the Vigilante Corps, who guard the island's natural resources and orient visitors. They told us of places of interest in Carite and were solicitous to the point of giving us the map off their wall. There are four picnic areas here, one camping area and many unmarked, overgrown trails — one of these trails leads to a waterfall, while another connects Cerro La Santa and a large natural pool, called Charco Azul.

We lunched at the Guavate picnic area across the road. Shelters and barbecue grills surrounding a pond are shaded by eucalyptus and royal palms. As we ate, a brief downpour drummed on the shelter roof and a hawk soared nearby, one of over 50 bird species sighted in Carite. The air was cool and damp (temperature averages 72 degrees).

Charco Azul

Río Patillas, a mere stream at this altitude, loops through a second picnic area, forming several small pools. A path enters the dim forest and follows the river, crossing it several times, before passing Charco Azul, reportedly the largest natural pool on the island. Some 30 feet wide and 20 feet deep, the pool has a bluish tinge due to the rock and soil formation of the riverbed. Visitors, mostly families, lounged in the shade, climbed rocks, waded or sipped beers. A rope swing dangles above the pool. Several boys performed a series of gymnastic leaps from the rope. One climbed a cliff next to the water. Headlines of "Boy Dies Impressing Female Travel Writer" flashed through my mind, but he jumped without incident.

Lago Carite

As we drove along a narrow road toward Lago Carite, a strange ghost development appeared on the side of the hills. A hundred brown and beige wood homes perched in various stages of abandonment. Apparently the builders of this white-elephant project went bankrupt. According to a local resident, the government was contemplating a "you cart the house away, it's yours" policy to clean up the hills (this could not be verified). On a subsequent visit, the road was closed to traffic at the entrance to the development. Visitors could still take a path to the lake edge.

The lake is an irregular shape of fingers stretching into forest on all sides. Most tropical lakes have a greenish hue from the profuse vegetation, but Carite looks almost blue. Few inhabited homes line the lake, and we noticed only one moored rowboat and two motorboats. A lakefront home owner assured us the lake is free of bilharzia-carrying snails, adding that his grandchildren swim here all the time. He felt the real danger lay in slipping into the water from the steep bank, ochre in color.

Several varieties of fish are stocked in Carite, and it is said to have the best bass fishing in Puerto Rico. Unfortunately, there are no boats or fishing equipment for rent. We sat beside the lake watching fish dive above the water and plop back again. Leaves arching toward the water gave off a pleasant smell. The air was silent.

Instead of camping

Beyond Lago Carite the mountains split, exposing broad views to Guayama and the south coast. We had planned to camp in the forest, but became so entranced by the views, the evening mists and the sunset, that night fell with its usual haste before we located a site. Instead, we opted for a more genteel alternative — dinner at the Jajome Terrace Restaurant before returning to San Juan.

Jajome Terrace is a converted country home, complete with stone verandah and pillars and latticed entranceway. The grounds are landscaped with a variety of tropical plants. Most impressive is the view toward the Caribbean.

Maunabo beach

We enjoyed a relish tray, soup and buffet dinner, then sat back with a cordial. **Coquís** kept up a pleasant racket. The distant lights of Salinas flickered in the darkness but did not tempt us to leave our mountain retreat, not just yet.

1990s UPDATE: If you want to drive the entire route with leisurely stops in one day, start early. Refer to a detailed highway map that highlights the Panoramic Route to get from Humacao to Yabucoa, around the coastal circuit, up to Carite and on to Cayey. The Punta Tuna lighthouse is no longer manned and will soon come under the care of the Conservation Trust. Land around Lago Carite has been developed, and you can reach the edge of the lake from Ramal 742 off the panoramic Route. Ask around about boats to rent. Ask at the ranger station (747-4545) about trails and their condition in Carite Forest. For camping, see the Vieques article; for more comfortable accomodations, try the Caribe Playa Resort (839-6339) along the coast in Patillas. Jájome terrace (Road 15, Km. 18.6, 738-4016) has been joined by several other good restaurants in the Cayey mountains, making it a popular region for weekend country dining. See **Qué Pasa** or other local tourism magazines for more information.

Puerto Rico's Ruta Panorámica, Carite Forest

Falls, Cañón San Cristóbal

SCRAMBLING THROUGH
SAN CRISTOBAL

A frothy ribbon of water slides off the juncture of two massive cliffs and plunges 60 feet into a pool. The pool is set on a small flood plain halfway up the wall of a deep canyon. Around the pool is a collection of melted metal "rocks," motors, chrome bumpers, springs and debris mixed with soil and tufts of grass.

The scene is part of Cañon San Cristóbal, five and a half miles of lush canyon between Aibonito and Barranquitas. It is the island's deepest gorge and, until six years ago, possibly the world's most incongruous garbage dump.

Aibonito

Early morning mists still lingered in the hills when we drove into Aibonito, a town encircled by mountains. Aibonito boasts the highest altitude and the lowest temperature (40 degrees F. in 1911) of any town on the island. In fact, barracks here were used, first by Spain, then by the U.S., to acclimate soldiers to Puerto Rico's tropical climate. In another historical distinction, Aibonito became the island capital for seven months in 1887 when General Palacios (one of Puerto Rico's more notorious governors) wanted to keep an eye on revolutionary rumblings in the mountains. Two versions exist explaining the town's euphonious name. In one, a Spanish gunman bushwhacking across the mountains in the early 1600's is said to have stopped at a summit overlooking the valley and exclaimed, "¡Ay, qué bonito!" (oh, how pretty). The Taíno Indians called this general area Atibonicu, "River of the Night;" some historians feel this is the correct derivation.

A high concentration of poultry farms and flower nurseries surrounds the town. In its plaza, we woke up with coffee at the Safari Park Restaurant and a view of the twin towers of a century-old Catholic church which have been struck, on separate occasions, by lightning. The church, wooden homes, pruned trees and a **botánica** selling medicinal herbs share the plaza with a more modern Methodist church, concrete buildings, telephone wires and a movie theater advertising John Travolta the day we were there.

A. Barranquitas B. Church, Aibonito plaza C. Farmer and tobacco shed near Cañón San Cristóbal

Skirting the canyon

Northwest of Aibonito a road skirts the eastern side of Cañon San Cristóbal, providing brief glimpses of upper canyon walls. A local resident argued that the canyon's highest waterfall — and at 100 feet probably the island's highest — located nearby is usually not as spectacular as a local commercial, taken after heavy rains, makes it to be. (I later visited the fall, and found it spectacular enough.) Another road faces the canyon, where we got our first view of the giant incision, puckered and nubby green, in the mountainous countryside. A third road parallels the Barranquitas side of the canyon. We entered Urbanización San Cristóbal after numerous inquiries; one man shook his head at our plan to descend the canyon: "It's steep..." he warned. The Lion's Club here overlooks the sprawling rift and a forked waterfall on the far side. Beyond the club, the road becomes a rutted lane, and wooden houses replace concrete ones.

The descent

The lane ends between a tobacco drying shed thatched with banana leaves and a furrowed field of young tobacco plants (on a later visit, cabbage had replaced tobacco). The Maldonado family permitted us to leave our car on their land. A woman was cutting grass with a machete. She pointed toward the trail, next to a rubber tree, adding that her family descended it daily to fish.

The trail switchbacks almost vertically through dry forest to the canyon floor. Rocks, roots and loose soil forced us to concentrate on our steps, not the surrounding views. Several hundred feet down, the vegetation darkens and a river "crescendos". Within a half hour we were resting under a legume tree at the bottom. Water flowed over numerous flat rocks. A hawk and several grassquits flew between 300-foot cliffs decked with **cupey** tree prop roots and a tangle of plants and grasses hardy enough to survive in the vertical cracks.

Two rivers merge in this area. We crossed one, entered a strip of forest and stepped onto the banks of the second. Upriver, somewhere between massive boulders and even more massive canyon walls, lay our "trail."

Surveying the canyon on an imaginary journey

If we endow ourselves with powers of the imagination and become a large **yagrumo** leaf swept into the water, we can travel along the entire length of the canyon. The leaf falls into a tributary in the area of Cerro Pulguillas (2,759 feet above sea level) near Coamo. Locally known as La Hoya de Aguas Largas (whirlpool of swift waters), the stream was used as a waterway to the Asomante community in Aibonito before the construction of a road.

A. *Wooden house on the plaza, Aibonito* B. *Cabbage patch near Cañón San Cristóbal*

Up here we float along a rugged route through coffee fields and dense forests before the stream passes hills cleared for cattle grazing. Several tributaries form a small lake; if we like, we can linger for a night under a dark constellation-studded sky. After drifting across the lake, past fields of cultivated flowers and peppers, we are pulled into a river, once named Honduras by the Spaniards, now known by the Indian word, Usabón.

The river meanders around hills until natural dams force the water to perform a series of spectacular drops. One drop is down the 100-foot fall mentioned earlier. Pools between cascades provide homes for freshwater fish and shrimp, as well as swimming holes, laundry basins and watering troughs for cattle smart — or foolish — enough to find the banks.

We are now in the main section of the canyon. Volcanic processes formed the cliffs during the Upper Mesozoic period, when dinosaurs were disappearing from North America and Puerto Rico was rising from the ocean. The canyon's formation was due to a set of faults which made it easier for the erosive process, begun when the island surfaced, to carve out gorges and precipices. Erosion carried away the sedimentary soil, leaving hardened lava in the shapes of hanging valleys, 700-foot cliffs, triangular facets and a rock profile of a giant face.

Tobacco, plantains and root plants grow on plots far above us, along the canyon rim. Native vegetation — such as climbing bamboo, strangler fig **(cupey)**, guava and short leaf fig **(jagüey blanco)** trees —clings to the cliff walls and banks of the river. Shrimp and filter feeders nibble at debris in the water. American kestrels **(falcón común)** and West Indian red-tailed hawks **(guaraguao)** circle overhead.

Our journey halts temporarily when the leaf gets lodged in the rusted door of a car pushed off the escarpment years ago. Until 1975 cars and other garbage from Aibonito and Barranquitas were conveniently shoved from view into the canyon. Much of the gorge was acquired by the Conservation Trust of Puerto Rico, and recently transferred to the Department of Natural Resources. Dumping is now prohibited, yet its vestiges are too costly and difficult to remove; fortunately, erosion and vines are gradually effacing the man-made blight.

Farther along, the Usabón widens with the addition of the Aibonito and Barranquitas rivers. The cliffs begin to decrease in height; soon the canyon is behind us. Near Comerío the Usabón merges with the larger Río de la Plata and makes its way to the Atlantic Ocean.

The real journey

"Trail" is a misnomer for the route we followed up the canyon. Hiking consisted of leaping over rocks in the river, squirming up egg-shaped boulders the size of rooms, slipping down mossy ledges and periodically pausing to decide the best way to continue. At times our efforts were facilitated by a well-dumped tire, a chassis, a rusted pulley. From the tops of boulders we viewed pools, stone formations, waterfalls and the canyon cliffs, rising more than 400 feet. Cactus limbs curved from cracks, and a lone **cupey** at the rim seemed to float in the sky.

At the juncture with one tributary (it must be obvious by now that. there are no identifying signposts) a 50-foot-high fall breaks over jagged rocks, forming a Cubist pattern. Several young men snorkeling for river shrimp assured us the water was free of bilharzia-carrying snails. We remained skeptical. By clambering up the right side of the fall, we reached the flood plain described at the start of the article. The movement of leaves marked the progress of one member of the expedition who entered tall weeds and fern brakes in an unsuccessful attempt to ascend a break in the cliffline for a view of a smaller upper fall.

A 12-foot-high waterfall plunges into a 40-foot-diameter pool farther ahead. The tan water is surrounded on three sides by ledges on which several boys scampered and jumped into the water. The only simple way to continue up the canyon is to swim across the pool. Most of the group did so, then continued over rocks, through thigh-deep water, around a cave, past vines of passion fruit **(parcha)** and squash, to a long pool decked with a tree felled by a recent storm.

Here the expedition split up. One person sat at the edge of the pool, drying jeans and matching birds with Peterson's **Field Guide.** Others floated across the pool on bamboo poles to view the narrowing chasm from the next boulder. The most energetic hiker forged ahead to where vegetation thickens, walls narrow and a 30-foot fall impedes further exploration without ropes.

Scenery blurred on the return trip as we hurried to beat a gathering storm back to the car. The bending, stretching, pulling, sliding and wedging occurred in fast motion. Rocks turned slippery, and sneakers seemed coated with grease. When we reached the car, the intermittent rain had become a downpour. We drove to Barranquitas; by the time we arrived the rain had stopped.

Barranquitas

The cream and burgundy San Antonio de Padua church tower and houses tightly clustered on several hills give Barranquitas a distinctly European look. This tidy, picturesque town is best known as the birthplace of Luis Muñoz Rivera, well-known island patriot, and as the resting place of Muñoz Rivera and his son, Luis Muñoz Marín, statesman and former governor of Puerto Rico. The well-tended grounds around the tombs also contain a modest museum. Next door, a small private museum houses an odd assortment of religious relics, Greek-Roman amphoras, the skeleton of a 12-year-old Taino boy from the Loíza area, and books by and about both Muñoz men. Near the plaza, the Muñoz Rivera museum, a quaint turn-of-the-century house, contains a small library of Puerto Rican and children's books. Also in the well-maintained museum are pieces of furniture and books from Muñoz Rivera's study, including a massive double desk, and a 1912 car used in his 1915 funeral procession.

When we left Barranquitas after our short visit, late afternoon mists fingered into the surrounding mountains. The day-and the trip-was almost over.

San Antonio de Padua church at Christmas time, Barranquitas

1990s UPDATE: There are undoubtedly reasons, most likely of an economical nature, that the plans for platforms overlooking San Cristóbal remain merely plans, but the canyon does deserve better. On the Aibonito side, a side road off Road 725, Km. 5.5, approaches the edge of the cliffs; ask neighbors about a cow path that becomes a trail to the 100-foot fall. On the Barranquitas side, Road 156, Km. 17.7, marks Urbanización San Cristóbal, where the Lion's Club provides the best panorama of the canyon. At the end of this urbanization (Calle A/G) is the trail we used to descend. I still do not recommend swimming in the river, more for reasons of possible sewage dumping than bilharzia (see the Toro Negro article).

A. *Butterfly* B. *Sierra palm prop roots*

ACROSS AND DOWN
TORO NEGRO

An all-night storm, complete with rain drumming on the roof, distant thunder and streaks of lightning, can arouse cozy and agreeable feelings, but not when it occurs on the eve of a weekend camping trip in Toro Negro.

Toro Negro Forest Reserve straddles the Cordillera Central, almost in dead center of the island. Its 7,000 acres include Puerto Rico's tallest peak and its highest lake, but most impressive to visitors are the spectacular views extending to the Atlantic and Caribbean, and the exotic lushness of the forest itself. Equally impressive to me that weekend were the numerous river sources hidden in the Cordillera Central's steep ridges, and I was later to make side trips down two of them.

A long stop at the Doña Juana Recreational Area

We stubbornly refused to give in to the whims of weather and drove to the reserve, halfway between Jayuya and Villalba, the next day. East of the forest entrance the road bisects the island. To the north, mountains plunge into karst hills which eventually level off to the Atlantic. Across the road they descend into khaki-colored plains around Ponce, with the Caribbean and Caja de Muertos island in the distance. This is one of the best places on the island to view both coasts from the same site.

Beyond the reserve entrance, a side road leads to the spindly Matrullas reservoir, the main road continuing on to the public recreational area at Doña Juana. Vegetation here is dense and wet; bamboo, ferns and trumpet trees **(yagrumo)** with floppy green and silver leaves stand out. Overhead, coal-colored clouds began to contest the patchy white ones that had been gathering.

A rocky path next to tall forest, pink impatiens and a stream connect the road with the recreational area. Picnic shelters with tables and barbecue pits border the Doña Juana pool, shaped in a sprawling "S." Its mountain stream water, though shallow and muddy, had enticed three local teenage boys. An overgrown trail leads to a stone lookout tower, an hour's hike away. The site has a not unpleasant feel of disuse, as if the forest were steadily reclaiming it.

A. *Swimming hole, Río Inabón* B. *Catching river shrimp* C. *Pool, Río Saliente* D. *Leaf study*

It is such tranquil abandonment that we did not mind when the deluge finally hit and we took cover in the bathhouse entrance. We did mind, though, when the rains continued for almost three hours (unloading 4.7 inches of water). Also trapped at the bathhouse was the pool lifeguard, who lives in the forest. Though he is 40, he looks 30 and has a body builder's physique. The rains (or the captive audience) got him talking, in rapid country Spanish, about his life, his big trip to San Juan for a body building contest 20 years earlier, and the forest.

The pool was built in the 1930's, when the Federal government administered Toro Negro as a division of the Caribbean National Forest (El Yunque). The forest looks primordial, yet most of the land had been cleared at some time in the past for cultivation. The Civilian Conservation Corps, which did extensive forestry work in Puerto Rico from 1935 to 1943, planted over 3 million tree seedlings and 19,000 pounds of seeds in Toro Negro. Troops training for the Korean War were stationed here, and National Guard soldiers in Salinas still come up for survival practice. In 1970 Toro Negro became part of the Puerto Rico forest reserve system.

The lifeguard spoke of freshwater shrimp he used to catch, which weighed as much as a pound and sold for a dime, and hikes down to Villalba. Meanwhile, rivulets of rain began flowing down the hills, the stream became a torrent and the pool rose eight feet in a half hour; excess brown water swirled over its far end. The lifeguard turned to local horror tales of chicken-eating dogs found dead, the murder of a silver dealer and death and injuries caused by just the sort of lightning as that flashing over our heads.

Of motels and quintas

When the rains let up (by no means stopping), we slipped down the path to the car and drove to the ranger station a mile farther west. The ranger shook his head at our camping plans, murmuring "tiempo fatal" (lousy weather) several times. The campsite, a small treeless field with several rustic gazebos, a picnic shelter and an outhouse, was slick with ochre-colored mud. The surrounding jungle dripped with moisture. Our camping plans dissolved into the drizzle.

Down the road a sign announcing rooms for rent, by week or month, marked a road leading up a hill hidden in thick fog. We hoped for the best, and drove up.

The owners of the rustic wood and metal A-frames on top of the hill were as wary of us as we were of them, barraging us with questions about our intentions before renting. This wariness relates to the concept of motels in Puerto Rico. For most North Americans the word **motel** conjures up images of unadorned lodgings next to highways, packed station wagons, yelling kids, undersized swimming pools. In Puerto Rico it evokes private garages leading to rooms, drinks and bills (calculated by the hour) appearing through slits in the doors, and lots of mirrors. In short, a rendezvous for extra-marital affairs.

Quinta (whose name studiously avoids the notorious word **motel**) Doña Juana is one of few lodgings for families and single people in the island's rural areas. It was built on a private tract of land within Toro Negro. Here we spent a pleasant, dry night. The owners and other guests visited us briefly. The rain stopped, mists cleared and lights from Villalba and Juana Díaz glimmered in a distant valley. A nearby bar played country music. **Coquí** frogs sang with such enthusiasm that reading proved difficult.

By morning, the temperature had dropped to 64 degrees (this was late September). Daylight created a vast collage of mountain slopes, peaks, valleys and sea. To the east is Cabañas de Doña Juana, a cluster of thatched **bohíos** where drinks and appetizers are served. A ten-minute walk up the lane across the road leads to an even more spectacular panorama that includes two manmade reservoirs — Lago Guayabal and Embalse Toa Vaca.

Landmarks hidden in forest

The section of the reserve west of Road 149 (where there is a community appropriately named Divisoria — the Divide) consists of dense forest blanketing mountain slopes. The most conspicuous tree, the sierra palm, has a thin trunk and ragged feathery leaves which create a cobweb texture on the upper slopes. These slow-growing palms do not bear coconuts. Even though they help prevent soil erosion, small landslides and forest debris littered the road after the previous day's storm.

Lago Guineo, highest lake on the island, is at the end of an unmarked side road. Occasional fish splashed through the lake's calm though murky surface. The lake, separated from the lower Río Toro Negro by a long dam, is fringed with thick bamboo and encircled by mountains. A local resident did not recommend swimming here, not so much because of possible bilharzia-carrying snails as because of the quicksand-like clay bottom.

From the Cerro Maravilla lookout, a 220-degree panorama exposes some 80 miles of south coast. At the communication tower on this peak two alleged saboteurs were killed by police several years ago. Though controversy surrounding their deaths still simmers, the site itself is placid and ruggedly beautiful. Unfortunately, its picnic area is in shambles.

A parking area devoid of signs marks the steep road to Cerro de Punta, highest peak on the island at 4,398 feet. On clear days points from San Juan to the west coast are seen from the top. Except for its several media towers and stations, the site instills viewers with an away-from-it-all invigoration.

Though our wet weekend trip ended with Cerro de Punta, my interest in Toro Negro did not, and I subsequently returned for closer looks at two of the seven rivers originating in this forest.

Terra incógnita: descending Inabón falls

From the moment I read of the spectacular waterfalls at Río Inabón, hidden somewhere in the rugged, remote southern half of Toro Negro, I was determined to see them. I soon had the good fortune to meet a man who had not only seen, but also descended them. Our meeting culminated in a trip, using ropes and the seats of our pants, down some 1,500 feet of cascading water, past plants and underbrush that surely had never been looked at by humans before.

The falls begin near the top of the Cordillera Central and end in a coffee plantation in Jurutungo near Ponce. To say a place "está por el Jurutungo" in Puerto Rico is to equate it with somewhere as remote as English's Timbuktu. Seen from below, the falls resemble mysterious vertical scabs — white with water after a heavy rain — between two mountain peaks.

The start of the trail leading to the Río Inabón — a mere brook at that altitude (4,000 feet) — is slightly west of Cerro Maravilla and difficult to locate. The first hour and a half of the trip consisted of easy hiking along the brook through rain forest vegetation. Rotting leaves and palm branches cover slick soil here. Moss grows everywhere — on rocks, on dead and living limbs, dangling from trees, on the ground, in the clear water. Tiny orchids and floppy bromeliads lodge in branch sockets. Dense foliage silhouettes the sky.

After the sounds of falling water become louder and the sky lighter, the world opens up. Miles of mountains brightened by salmon-colored tree blossoms curve into the plains around Ponce, with the Caribbean beyond. Immediately below, jagged boulders and waterfalls descend almost vertically out of view into sierra palm forest.

For the next six hours we doubled our rope around trees and descended cliff after cliff of rock and underbrush. The river forms about 15 major falls — some spindly, others squat, averaging 30 feet — and numerous smaller drops. Boulders, weeds and occasional bright flowers line the falls. Forest is everywhere else. Roots and vines tangled about us, and loose dirt irritated our eyes. Muscles tired from the strain and nervousness, and we moaned at the announcement of "another vertical precipice." Once when we crossed a gully next to an especially high fall, loose dirt slipped out from beneath three pairs of feet, and we dangled from the rope like a bulky version of Chinese paper fish. Careening rocks barely missed several heads.

The river finally leveled out at the site of a large, deep pool with a waterfall, 60-degree water, river shrimp, cliffs on three sides, diving ledges and a rock beach — in short, the ideal swimming hole. An hour and a half of hiking along the river remained beyond the swimming hole. Here pools stretch out in a montage of differing sizes and shapes; all have individual waterfalls. Strangler figs **(cupey)** with pendulous roots and other trees cram the river banks. In one section, algae-reddened boulders form a natural rollercoaster slide into a chasm partly filled with dark water.

A. *Coffee hacienda in the Cordillera Central near Jayuya* B. *Dam, Lago Guineo*

The beauty of the scene was lost on us in our exhaustion. When we turned at last onto an old coffee trail — the first hint of civilization since we started — no one was tempted to search for a nearby abandoned shack where coffee was once processed. All marched like robots to the welcoming party at the end of the trail.

Following the source

When you watch a river move through a city before entering the sea — often sluggish, oil-filmed, dun-drab, lined with asphalt, buildings, rusting boats, old tires — it is hard to imagine its pristine origins.

We returned to Toro Negro soon after the Inabón descent, locating the source of the Río Saliente and following it for several miles to the Coabey community east of Jayuya. This small river merges with several others to eventually become part of the Río Grande de Arecibo, which ends at the city of the same name.

The Saliente originates slightly east of Monte Jayuya (between Cerro de Punta and Cerro Maravilla), in uninhabited forest. At the road, mountain grass gave off a pungent smell and several hawks **(guaraguao)** circled overhead, screeching like cats in pain. We slid down a grassy incline to enter the crepuscular forest, full of sierra palm prop roots, rotting branches and moist, mossy rocks. Our sneakers landed ankle-deep in drenched soil — the emergence of one tributary of the river.

As we descended, boulders increase in size and small falls lengthen. Dense vines give the illusion of falling rain. Beetles tumbled in small pools. A walking stick insect wore a mossy camouflage coat. Roots and trunks provided leverage on the slick river banks.

As the river widens, sunlight increases and the vegetation looks dryer. We seemed to be playing a game of giant hopscotch as we stepped from rock to rock in the water. Waterfalls soon thicken and plunge into a necklace of pools. We swam across a cold 30-foot one in teeth-chattering style to discover a smaller "jacuzzi" pool next to a waterfall.

The remains of a small dam (once part of a watermill), a barely perceptible trail, numerous coffee bushes, a skeletal shack and several deserted houses are part of an abandoned community. Though we imagined a mysterious tragedy — an epidemic, a massacre — the buildings most likely housed coffee workers who left the timeless beauty of the mountains for greater opportunities. Yet another building — once a barn and coffee processing shed, now missing boards and doors, lacking water and electricity — housed a young couple who, with their daughter, three dogs and a duck, left the greater opportunities of San Juan in part for the timeless beauty of the mountains.

A jeep road, which winds through bananas, avocado and orange trees, led us to the main road, and our ride home.

1990s UPDATE: All Toro Negro Forest highlights are off Road 143 (I traveled from east to west); some still require perseverance to find. Check at the ranger station (867-3040) for a map of forest trails and for current condition of the Doña Juana pool and the lookout tower trail. A site I have missed, with regret, is Chorro Doña Juana, a popular mountain cascade off Road 149 near 143. Apparently, the **quinta** and **cabañas** are still there, and the picnic area near Cerro Maravilla has been repaired. The river descents should be attempted only by experienced wilderness hikers, who should let the rangers know their intentions. The starts of both descents are found through exploratory trial and error, though a topographical map (second floor, Minillas south building, 721-8787) helps. For information about camping, see the Karst country article. Turn of-the-century lodgings are in Jayuya at Parador Hacienda Gripiñas (828-1717). There is a lovely, rarely, used network of road, coffee lanes and paths that connects the **parador** with Cerro de Puntas.

A NOTE ABOUT BILHARZIA: Bilharzia is an infection found throughout the tropics. It is caused by Schistosoma, whose larvae are developed in the water snail Biomphalaria. The snail itself is not dangerous except when infected from human excrement. The acute symptoms of bilharzia resemble typhoid. Though it rarely kills its victims, it damages the liver and produces a general malaise which can last for decades. Drug treatment is still not satisfactory. The bilharzia infection rate dropped from about 15 percent of the Puerto Rican population in the 1930's to about five percent in the 1970's due to migration to the cities, rural aqueducts and snail control. However, the snail remains widely distributed in all types of freshwater habitats, and there is no guarantee that water contact is safe anywhere. Yet many people (including myself) swim and even drink water in the swift-running mountain streams above human habitation, feeling those areas are safe from infected snails. Few dare to swim in slower waters at lower elevations. Each visitor will have to make his or her own decision on the matter.

BEACHES AND BIRDS
IN GUANICA

Guánica Forest west of Ponce is a dry forest that is nevertheless always green. In spite of a scarcity of water, it supports the richest bird population on the island and boasts a lignum vitae tree more than half a millennium old, possibly the oldest of its species in Puerto Rico. U.S. troops first landed in Puerto Rico at Guánica's bay in 1898. Central Guánica, once one of the largest sugar mills on the island, now closed, still retains its machinery and turn-of-the-century ambiance. Yet most visitors to the area ignore all this, preferring instead Guánica's beaches, which are some of the finest on the southern coast. We tried to see everything.

The hills

A narrow road winds past subtropical dry vegetation into the upland areas of the forest reserve. Though the underbrush is dusty and bromeliads on limbs resemble birds' nests more than their fleshy rain forest counterparts, the forest is green, due in part to its lignum vitae **(guayacán)** trees. Lignum vitae (Latin for wood of life) are identified by small blue flowers and dense foliage that remains deep green even in dry spells. The heavy, slow-growing wood has been used in medicines and machinery construction. In addition to the lignum vitae, some 700 other plant species grow in Guánica — a few grow nowhere else in the world. Birds flock to this floral potpourri: half of all terrestrial bird species found in Puerto Rico are represented in Guánica, making it a mecca for bird watchers. The Puerto Rican whippoorwill **(guabairo)**, for eighty years considered extinct, was rediscovered in Guánica in 1951 and now boasts some 300 breeding pairs.

Limestone rocks poke out of the soil near the ranger station, and cacti and spreading acacia **(aroma)** trees contribute to the dry look of the landscape. The main picnic area is set in the ruins of a Spanish military camp, but it (and most of the reserve) is barely developed. An unusual cave in the area was carved out of lime soil as penance by employees of the Civilian Conservation Corps. Built for use during hurricanes, it was apparently more often used as a place for informal jailings. Its beige tunnels look like something out of Gaudí's architecture.

A. *Guánica* B. *Vulture, Babía de la Ballena* C. *Library, Ensenada*

Three jeep roads (not always open to vehicles, though always open to feet) fan into the forest. The road southeast of the ranger station is the best for viewing birds in the very early morning. Another passes near the ancient lignum vitae tree. That tree, between 500 and 700 years old, is only about two feet in diameter — proof of lignum vitae's slow growth. The third road leads to a stone tower in excellent condition which was used by Spaniards during the 1898 war. From here visitors get a broad view of the town and bay of Guánica. Back at the ranger station, a trail passes several shortleaf fig trees with aerial root streamers (but no edible figs) on its way to a bat cave, now apparently without bats. None of these sites is marked, in part for reasons of preservation.

The towns

The town of Guánica is nestled around a bulge in the doorknob-shaped bay. In addition to a lovely central plaza, there is an attractive sea wall lined with benches where people can promenade or just rest. Midway along the wall a plaque donated by the Puerto Rican chapter of the Daughters of the American Revolution and a boulder donated by the town (both remarkably intact) commemorate the landing of U.S. troops under General Nelson A. Miles on July 25, 1898, during the Spanish-American War. To the east, high above the Ochoa fertilizer factory, is the tower visited earlier, from which Spanish troops most likely observed the landing.

To the west, at the far end of the bay, the town of Ensenada surrounds Central Guánica. Up until recently, the sweet stench of sugar cane processing permeated the town from February to June, when clanging machines worked 24 hours a day to process cane into juice and then into sugar. Bin-shaped trucks stuffed with sugar cane lined up to be weighed on huge scales. A wage dispute terminated operation of the mill, although sugar production has been a money-losing venture on the island for some time.

Yet the buildings and machinery remain intact, as do several fashionable mill houses. With their verandahs and spacious lawns, they seem to represent a North American's idea of genteel tropical living in the early 1900's. Most picturesque is a one-room library, completely surrounded by a verandah that looks bigger than the building.

The beaches

Calm water, patches of mangrove, scrub vegetation and hot, sunny skies distinguish the numerous beaches on both sides of Guánica's bay. To the east, the road curves around cliffs at the neck of the bay. Playa Jaboncillo, a well-hidden cove, lies at the bottom of the cliffs; the skeletal remains of a vandalized lighthouse are at the top. The road returns to sea level and passes a long strip of public bathing beach at Caña Gorda. Beyond the modern Hotel Copamarina there are no more developments, only mangrove cays off Punta San Jacinto, tiers of dry forested hills and scalloped coastline.

Coconut palm forest and low-lying mangroves share a prominent delta-shaped extension east of the hotel. Next to it another long beach rims Bahía de la Ballena (whale bay). Arches of lava rock jut into the sea. At Playa Tamarindo, where the facilities were run down the last time I visited, shells and shell fragments line the beaches and sea bottom in places. Pelicans joined us in the water as we swam. A local visitor mentioned that similar beaches, divided by rocky outcrops and good for snorkeling, extend along the coast to Bahía de Guayanilla. They are only accessible by jeep, or foot.

The dirt road leading to the Guánica Forest reserve beaches west of Guánica bay is pocked with rocks and streaked with washed out gullies. The first time I visited, a member of the (now defunct) Young Adult Conservation Corps explained that hurricanes had worsened the road, but that within two months they hoped to have it improved. When I returned two years later, it was in the same condition. Although cars do reach the beaches, we feared it would be at great expense to exhaust systems and oil pans, and preferred to walk.

As the road ascends into low-lying hills, it approaches a large lagoon separated from an even larger bay by a mere strip of sand and palms. The road forks, the left branch cutting through shrub forest that has touches of red and brown mixed with the dominant green, the right branch continuing on to the beaches.

The most impressive feature of the first beach we reached — Manglillo Grande — was its array of colors. Pale green leaves topped tangles of gray mangrove limbs. Citron green grasses, dried seaweed and brown sticks spotted curves of bone-colored sand. Pale blue water darkened at the horizon, yet was lighter than the storm clouds and waterspout above the sea.

Campers at Manglillo Grande informed us that the second popular beach in this area — Manglillo Pequeño — was on the other side of a hill extending to the sea. We followed a footpath over jagged rocks. Fifteen minutes later we stepped onto a small curve of beach similar to the first. A clump of mangrove seemed to float some fifty feet offshore. We were surprised to see several families scattered along the sand and in the water. This supposedly "inaccessible" beach is actually quite near a residential road.

In contrast to the Manglillo beaches, what was most distinctive about Playa Santa, our last stop, was the absence of colors. We arrived after the sun had set. The beach and clouds were mere black silhouettes, the sky a deep salmon pink and the sea a reflection of the sky. A group played volleyball, oblivious to the mosquitoes, as the last bit of light faded away.

Stone tower, Guánica Forest B. Manglillo Pequeño beach C. Tunnel through chalk soil, Guánica Forest

1990s UPDATE: The Guánica Forest Reserve has received modest publicity in the past several years. An increasing interest in eco-tourism has resulted in greater interest in Guánica's natural distinctions, which some time ago earned the forest the designation of a United Nations Biosphere Reserve. Road 334 (south) east of town leads to the hilly section of the reserve and the ranger station. Road 333 skirts the eastern coastal section of the reserve. Road 325 from Ensenada west of downtown Guánica passes through the western coastal section of the reserve and continues to Playa Santa in the community of Salinas. There is no longer camping in the forest, but the bird watching remains excellent (see the Karst Country and Culebra articles). Mary Lee's by the Sea (821-3600) continues to cater to those who enjoy nature, and the Hotel Copamarina (821-0505) has become one of the island's most popular small resorts.

A. *Plaza, Maricao* B. *Coffee shrub* C. *Charco el Mangó*

THE HEART OF THE HEART OF
COFFEE COUNTRY

The best-known features of the Maricao Forest on the western slopes of the Cordillera Central are an observation tower, a vacation center and a fish hatchery. A historical event turned legend distinguishes Guilarte Forest, slightly to the east of Maricao. Yet both forests are most appreciated by those who know them for what they do **not** have. Little has been developed in either reserve. Trails lead into untouched expanses of forest. Birds, frogs and faraway roosters interrupt the silence — not motors, machines nor crowds of people. And on the drive connecting the two reserves visitors pass through mountainous coffee country little affected by today's progress.

A look at the best-known features of the Maricao area

Maricao, north of the forest reserve, is officially the smallest town on the mainland in Puerto Rico with some 3,000 residents (smaller communities are **barrios** in a larger municipality). From a distance, faded wooden homes with cast iron balconies and small concrete stores seem to hibernate on the sides of the mountains. A beige church with its red steeple dominates the town's skyline.

Parador Hacienda Juanita west of town is a coffee estate converted into a tranquil country inn. Its wide verandah lies between a lounge and dining room — where ceiling beams of **ausubo** wood date back to the plantation's original construction in 1830 — and lush, well-tended gardens. Coffee relics decorate these rooms, and a mill on the site still operates during the week. A trail below the buildings skirts citrus trees, coffee bushes and a stream. A meditation park overlooking Maricao and its chalk-white cemetery and a grotto sanctuary of St. John the Baptist are a short drive from the **parador.**

Within the Maricao Forest Reserve, established in 1919, a sign leading to Casa de Piedra, a rustic stone mountain house, also leads to a camping area which I consider the nicest in the forest reserve system. A level, sparsely forested field overlooks a fishbowl view of southwest Puerto Rico. Campers have access to running water, one large roofed picnic area and an outhouse. Nights are chill (in winter, temperatures drop into the 50's) and their pristine blackness is rarely broken by more than specks of fireflies, stars and towns glimmering in the valleys.

A 40-foot stone observation tower, built in the 1930's by the Civilian Conservation Corps, shares the high point in the forest (2,625 feet) with several communications antennae. From the tower, three sides of Puerto Rico and Mona island, 50 miles away, are seen on clear days.

East of the tower is the Monte del Estado Vacation Center, an attractive complex of cabins, swimming pool, basketball court and cafeteria. Wood and concrete cabins accommodate up to six people, who must provide sheets, towels and utensils. Inexpensive to rent, the cabins are usually reserved more than three months in advance on weekends. Nearby, a large picnic area surrounded by citrus trees and bamboo narrows into a path bordered by a shrine to the Virgin Mary. From the lookout at the path's end, a slanting expanse of forest resembles the Great Smokey Mountains.

The Fish Hatchery trail

The Fish Hatchery trail connects the Maricao ridge with a fish hatchery some 1,350 feet below. I hiked this little-used trail with Julio Figueroa, who works at the Institute of Tropical Forestry, in just under seven hours, making many stops along the way. The trail begins inauspiciously at Km. 14.8 on Road 120. There is no sign indicating the trailhead, only a **caimitillo** tree with dense, deep green foliage on the left and a pile of rocks at the entrance.

Much of the rock in this area is bluish-green hued serpentine, a magnesium and iron silicate of submarine volcanic origin. Although soils derived from this rock are low in basic nutrients, high in toxic magnesium and among the poorest on the island for agriculture, the natural vegetation here is, oddly enough, known for its great diversity and high percentage of endemic (native) species. Of 278 tree species in Maricao — more than in any other individual reserve on the island — 123 do not grow outside Puerto Rico, 110 are rare or endangered and 37 are found only in this forest. Because of man's lack of interest in cultivating such poor soil, large areas of the reserve have remained virgin forest, a condition which less than one percent of the island can claim.

The trail follows the ridge of the mountain. Leaves here are small and brittle, tree ferns have dried up, spindly trumpet tree **(yagrumo)** trunks support little foliage. Mountaintop winds and the extremely permeable serpentine cause this stintedness. In spite of a large amount of rainfall, the Maricao forest resembles dry karst vegetation more than that of the rain forests.

Birds enliven the otherwise silent forest. Maricao is one of the best places on the island for watching resident birds. There are more than 44 species here, including the Puerto Rican woodpecker **(carpintero de Puerto Rico)** scaly-naped pigeon **(paloma turca),** Puerto Rican tody **(San Pedrito)** and four species of hawks, two of which — the broad-winged **(guaraguao de bosque)** and the sharp-skinned **(falcón de sierra)** — are rare and endangered.

Its diversity of vegatation also makes Maricao interesting to tree watchers. Trees are identified by the arrangement of leaves on leaf stalks, or petioles, and the arrangement of stalks on stems. In addition, botanists use hand lenses to examine the textures of leaves. Figueroa identified one sapling as a member of the Myrtaceae (myrtle) family; by crushing its leaf and releasing an aromatic smell, he further deduced the sapling was an **ausú** tree **(Pimenta racemosa grisea)** known for its aromatic oil, a close relative of the bay rum used in cosmetics and medicines. By using these techniques, he and I became a botanical Holmes-Watson team, identifying numerous trees as well as several common plants which cause painful rashes.

About a mile into the forest, where the ridge shades denser, moister vegetation, the trail performs a series of disappearing acts. It is hidden under tangles of grasses and rotting logs, or covered by small landslides, or cut by streams descending to the Río Maricao. Yet we always found it again after several minutes of anxious bushwhacking.

The forest became taller, with most leaves now far above us and the undergrowth less dense, as we left the lower montane wet forest and entered the subtropical wet forest. Predominant **tabonuco** trees, buttressed **granadillo** trees and species of the mahogany, laurel and pepper families characterize this forest zone. The **moralón** tree found here, (named grand leaf seagrape in English, in part for its fanlike round leaves) branches out like trees in a Japanese print.

In the Río Maricao valley, where the river flows in a wide bed parallel to the trail, the forest takes on a jungly quality. Rotten yellow fruits of the **jácana** tree line the trail. Yellow and red bracts of heliconia add color. Vanilla orchids and philodendron vines swing from tree limbs. We arrived in this area around 4:00 p.m. Ominous thunderclaps, a darkening sky and a din of crickets heralded the monsoon-like shower, typical on summer afternoons, that engulfed us to the end of the trail near the fish hatchery.

The Fish Hatchery

The Maricao Fish Hatchery is the only freshwater hatchery in Puerto Rico and the sole source of 15,000 to 26,000 fish dumped yearly into 26 lakes and 70 farm fish ponds around the island. A variety of fish including black bass, channel catfish, sunfish, peacock bass from Colombia and tilapias from Africa are hatched in breeding ponds and raised in growing tanks, then netted and delivered free of charge to the various lakes. The purpose of the hatchery is to provide a nutritious variety of fish to sport fishermen. Fernando Villa Romero, technician at the hatchery almost since its inception in 1938, mentioned that the site, in addition to breeding fish, functions as an educational and scientific center in a pleasant surrounding for visitors.

The setting is pleasant. An assortment of concrete tanks — circular, cell-shaped, shallow, deep — hold schools of sashaying fish. Well-tended gardens surround the pools and tanks (picnics are not permitted). Forested hills and the Río Maricao border the grounds.

A. *Campsite, Guilarte Forest* B. *Tanks, Maricao Fish Hatchery* C. *Coffee hacienda near Castañer* D. *Helicon*

Coffee country

The island's Ruta Panorámica connects the Maricao and Guilarte forest reserves along back roads that wind through the heart of Puerto Rico's coffee country. Late autumn is harvesting time. Arching tree crowns and tattered plantain leaves shade steep plantations of deep-green coffee shrubs and ripened red beans. Along the narrow, twisting lanes, coffee drying on burlap spread on the pavement is as common as laundry drying on bushes, necessary improvisations in such rugged country. The fleshy berries around the beans soften in giant vats inside small roadside mills. Citrus trees line the roadways.

Southwest of the reserve is Castañer, also called Los Rábanos, the quintessential mountain community where horses still clop down the one main road. Country music replaces **salsa** on the radio, men congregate outside small bars, homes are scattered along a valley clefted by a small river. Above, the hills are thick with coffee and patches of pine forest. The community's pride is Castañer General Hospital, founded in 1942 by conscientious objectors from the Church of the Brethren; it is the island's only rural mountain hospital, serving six neighboring municipalities.

Near Castañer, hidden at the end of a nameless lane encroached on by ferns and plantain leaves, set in the folds of misty hills, is an old coffee plantation, one of several in the area. Coffee has not been picked here commercially for two decades, and the land has an abandoned, overgrown look. A water-driven turbine, depulping machine, metal dryer, roller crusher and an assortment of concrete troughs, old saddles, straw baskets and rusted cans are relics inside a mill of wood and galvanized iron; these objects seem tinted the sepia tones of old photographs.

Indigenous to Ethiopia, coffee was brought to the Caribbean (Martinique) by a French officer. From the early 1700's until 1898 it was a main Puerto Rican export, especially to Spain and Europe. Then the devastating Hurricane San Ciriaco destroyed many coffee plantations, and the Spanish-American War resulted in the loss of the Spanish market. In ensuing years, social changes led to workers' reluctance to pick for meager wages and further decline in coffee production. Though there is currently a revival in coffee growing, using nets, fertilizers and other work-efficient practices to produce extremely high yields, many of the old haciendas — picturesque but unable or unwilling to change their traditional methods — have ceased production.

Guilarte Forest Reserve

Six separate tracts of land make up the 3,600-acre Guilarte Forest Reserve several miles west of Castañer. Lush crowded forest covers rugged slopes. Citrus trees coexist with sierra palms in ravines teeming with vegetation; dwarf forest covers the highest peaks and wind-exposed ridges.

A. *Eucalyptus, Guilarte Forest* B. *Coffee hacienda near Castañer* C. *Lizard on trunk*

The forest's isolated, natural state is altered only by two picnic areas and a campsite near the ranger station. In the picnic areas, plants surround rustic stick tables, benches and gazebo shelters. Overhead, tall, slender trees with delicate leaves and bark resembling cracked leather form part of a 350-acre eucalyptus plantation. Lookouts face forested mountainsides and the whitened buildings of Adjuntas, some six miles to the east.

There are actually two campsites at Guilarte, although one is merely a grassy area on a mountain slope. The main site resembles a miniature Taino Indian village of round and square wooden huts set on the upward slope of two ravines. Campers share a faucet, an outhouse and a makeshift shower of cold mountain water. A precipitous dirt road descends to the site. When filled, the area lacks privacy, for hut doors face each other. Black tangles of vegetation and eucalyptus trunks obscure the sky at night. When we camped here, myriad crickets and **coquí** frogs lulled us to sleep, and battalions of mosquitoes and distant roosters woke us up.

The few trails that once penetrated the forest are now unmarked and overgrown. Only the Monte Guilarte trail remains intact. It is a steep, half-hour hike on slick red clay soil. Drizzle and shade shroud sierra palms, **yagrumo**, ferns, coleus and lovely patches of pink impatiens. From the open, rocky summit, the view encompasses ridges, valleys, fields, lakes, communities and sea. A lack of the usual mountaintop towers and transmitters ensures uninterrupted tranquillity.

The gold nugget

Displayed in a picnic area announcement box is the short story "El grano de oro" written by Cayetano Coll y Toste and based on the local legend which gives the mountain its name.

The gist of the tale is that Orozco, pale-faced and greedy, convinces his friend Guilarte, dark-skinned and good-humored, to cross the island in search of gold. The year is 1530. When they arrive at what is now Monte Guilarte, Guilarte spies a large chunk of gold-filled quartz in a ravine, and they fashion a ladder of bark and vines to retrieve it. Orozco decides the nugget is not big enough for both of them and challenges Guilarte to a throw of the dice to decide who will keep the gold. Orozco wins. Guilarte congratulates him, then returns to the summit. As Orozco climbs up the ladder, it breaks and he plunges into the dense underbrush. There he lies, with two broken legs, clutching the nugget. Guilarte scrambles back to Caparra, returning a week later with Indian friends in time to hear Orozco's dying confession that the dice were loaded. Guilarte donates the nugget to the Cathedral in Seville, and the king gives him all the land he and Orozco, dead due to avarice, had explored. The moral is clear.

Things have changed since Guilarte's day. The trip can now be made in a fraction of the time, but there is little hope of spying a quartz chunk glinting with gold.

Side excursions

Northeast of the reserve is Charco el Mangó, a natural pool along a tributary of the Río Blanco. The 40-foot-wide, cliff-lined pool is bordered by vines and thicket. It is a popular local swimming hole, rarely found by visitors. Southeast of the reserve, Garzas dam, built more than 40 years ago, has created the Lago Garzas reservoir. The lake is a graceful collection of green-hued fingers extending into bamboo-fringed forest. A huge tunnel at one stem of the lake funnels water to the south coast.

Beyond the dam is Adjuntas, mountain town and center of coffee and citron cultivation. The Monte Río Hotel, off the town's baroque plaza, provides guests with modest rooms and small terraces facing the mountains. Good country food is served in its restaurant. While there, we learned that Adjuntas is nicknamed "Town of the Sleeping Giant" because of the reclining shape of the mountains in the background. We sensed another legend waiting patiently to be immortalized by a contemporary Coll y Toste.

1990s UPDATE: Those who want to see an old-time coffee estate should visit Hacienda Buena Vista off Highway 10 (km. 16.8) near Ponce. Nicely restored by the Conservation Trust of Puerto Rico, the farm showcases functioning coffee and corn mills. Reservations are required to visit the site; call 722-5882. Although many of the old estates continue to weather on the mountain slopes, the new farms are doing well and even producing gourmet blends which are being sold internationally and in local shops. In addition to coffee, Adjuntas produces citron, a curious fruit primarily known as an ingredient in fruitcakes. To get to most places, buy a detailed highway map that includes the panoramic Route. Charco el Mangó is off road 525; ask. Hacienda Juanita in Maricao (838-2550) remains a pleasant parador. The Monte Río Hotel (829-3705) is still in Adjuntas, where there is also the family-oriented Villas de Sotomayor (829-5105). Contact the Department of Recreation and Sports (722-1551) about the Maricao Monte del Estado Vacation Center. Unfortunately, camping is no longer permitted in the Maricao Forest, and only the wooden huts are available to campers in Guilarte (see the Karst County article). The Fish Hatchery Trail apparently remains unmaintained; check at the ranger stattion if you are interested.

A NOTE ABOUT THE RUTA PANORAMICA: Road 105 in Mayagüez marks the western start of the Ruta Panorámica, a 165-mile network of 40 roads which meanders across the island's mountains to the southeast town of Yabucoa. The route offers views of unspoiled tropical beauty, modest prices, and the experience of rural Caribbean living. In exchange, travelers must become explorers, armed with a detailed highway map, for the route and specific points of interest are often unmarked. In places the roads are so tortuous that some recommended Dramamine. Allow three days to travel the entire route leisurely. There are numerous **colmados** (for refreshments and snacks) and several restaurants along the way. Recommended lodging can be found in Mayagüez, Maricao, Adjuntas, Jayuya and Patillas (again, see **Qué Pasa**). In Aibonito, the owner of La Piedra Restaurant (735-1034) hopes to open a hotel, and the Sand and Sea Restaurant in Cayey (738-9086) has rooms for overnight stays. See also the chapters on Toro Negro, San Cristóbal and southeast Puerto Rico.

Moon through bougainvillea, Hacienda Juanita

House off the plaza, San Germán

IN AND AROUND PARGUERA

Two small fishing boats chugging across a gentle, moonlit sea represented for me the best-known aspects of Parguera. One boat carried a lone fisherman: Parguera was, and still is, a fishing village. The second boat carried 18 passengers to Bahía Fosforescente, the best-known of Puerto Rico's phosphorescent bays.

In addition, Parguera makes an ideal starting place to visit a number of other landmarks in the semiarid southwestern corner of Puerto Rico. A still functioning salt farm, a lighthouse, a mile-long beach, bizarre rock formations and the island's second oldest town are within an hour's drive of Parguera on back roads which can be adventures in themselves.

To the town

A back road connecting Guánica with Parguera passes landscapes that resemble ghost town country in the U.S. West. Hills are parched under an incessant sun. Mesquite trees and cacti shade thin cattle near water troughs and small windmills. Wooden houses, some on stilts, some abandoned, are scattered along the road. Goats wander freely. Deserted evaporation pools which produce sea salt give off an assortment of hues: iridescent ochre, glossy peach, milky silver.

The town itself

Parguera, with its numerous houses and wide expanse of sea, is a pleasant contrast to the desolate back road. All roads fan into the hub of the town — its plaza and dock area. Though set between hills and sea, most houses face the sea. One hill — Las Colinas, site of an abandoned building — surveys the town, the "squatter" shacks lining the bay (much mangrove forest has been destroyed building these shacks, most of which are weekend homes), dozens of cays of various sizes and flocks of birds. This is a fine place to watch a sunrise or sunset. Below, several shops sell souvenirs, and The Beachcomber offers locally made crafts. A small museum, The Shell Mound, displays an international shell collection.

Local entertainment on land centers around several clean, well-maintained seafood restaurants. Foods range from **empanadillas** (stuffed turnovers) at **cafeterías** to Sunday buffet at the Villa Parguera

A. *Mangrove cays, Parguera* B. *Cabo Rojo lighthouse* C. *Railroad tunnel, Guaniquilla*

A. *Inside the Camuy cave, Tres Pueblos entrance*

B. *Buyé beach near Boquerón*   C. *Rimstone pools, the Camuy cave (photo by Garred Giles)*

D. *Sierra palms and hiker, Luquillo mountains*

E. *Railroad tunnel near Boquerón* F. *Orchids, Botanical Garden, Río Piedras*

G. Picnic area, Guilarte Forest H. *Upper Río Espíritu Santo* I. *Heliconia, El Yunque*

J. *Falls, Cañón San Cristóbal*   K. *Mangrove channel, Parguera*   L. *Fishing boat, Maunabo beach*

ijardo marina N. *Botanical Garden, Río Piedras* O. *Fungi near the Río Tanamá* P. *Sooty terns, Culebra*
* onal Wildlife Refuge (photo by Kathryn Robinson)*

Q. *Balneario Lucia near Yabucoa, view to Vieques*

Hotel, the town's best-known lodging and part of the **parador** system. We stopped at the Dead End Restaurant at the western edge of town for an excellent fish dinner. The place is well named; beyond it, a dirt road leads to the former town dump, a swampland sprouting rusted cars, soggy mattresses and a sea of broken glass, impressive in its way. Several bars in town cater to the thirsty. The Karacol Bar is said to host stimulating conversations among off-duty naturalists, geologists, ichthyologists and psychologists from Mayagüez UPR's Experiment Station on Isla Magüeyes just off Parguera.

During the week Parguera is a tranquil, slow-moving place, sparsely populated with visitors in shorts and T-shirts. On weekends, the town fills up with families and young couples from all over the island; the pace is faster and noisier. There is discotheque dancing as well as an orchestra and midnight shows at the Villa Parguera Hotel.

The surrounding sea

The passengers in both boats mentioned at the start of this article would have preferred a moonless night: for the fishermen it would have meant a larger catch, for the visitors a more spectacular bioluminescence in Bahía Fosforescente. The glow is caused by billions of microscopic dinoflagellates which light up when disturbed by movement and provide a glittering psychedelic lightshow. It is a phenomenon limited to protected shorelines in tropical waters, and then only under certain conditions, such as moonless nights. The night we were there, when the moon was full and haloed, we had to content ourselves with splashing at water shaded by the boat and watching modest sparkles fall back into the bay. Yet the boatride through various shades of darkness — a glossy sea, a flat-textured sky, smoke-gray clouds, black cays and hills — was pleasurable in itself.

During the day, fishing is one of the most popular sports at Parguera. Fishermen can rent a boat, or merely throw a line at the end of a rickety dock, and wait for a bite from any of an assortment of fish, from barracuda to **pargo** (a type of snapper that gives the town its name).

Visitors can snorkel and swim at Playa Rosada and Isla Mata de la Gata, both equipped with picnic facilities, which are part of a forest reserve of mangrove swamp that extends along the coast from Parguera to Boquerón. Playa Rosada is a small beach east of town. A walkway here is lined with lignum vitae trees, and a path leads over a hill to a cove. Isla Mata de la Gata, named for cats once found on it, is a mangrove cay about two miles from shore. Boats regularly transport visitors from town to the island. The sandy part of this island is so small it can be crossed in one breath. Mangroves extend into the sea and a long dock encloses a triangle of shallow, protected water for bathers. Though the island and Playa Rosada are both lovely spots, their recent development was accompanied by an unfortunate circumstance: wastes discharged from homes lining the bay have polluted the waters nearer to town.

More than 30 mangrove islands dot the bay. Boats can be rented to explore the islands, the channels separating them and the surrounding sea life (including such oddities as sea porcupines and coral dusters that disappear when touched). In one particularly beautiful stretch near Isla del Mono (once overrun by monkeys being studied), mangrove limbs form ornate archways over narrow canals. We felt we had somehow strayed to the edge of a magical kingdom.

To the lighthouse

"The shortest route is not always the fastest" is a saying that came to mind as we took the back road from Parguera to the Cabo Rojo lighthouse. The road, a dotted line on our map, is dirt and was sprinkled with large puddles and rocky inclines — more appropriate for a jeep than the car we drove. In spite of some tight spots, we enjoyed the challenges of such a little-traveled road and the views of pastures sloping into a distant sea. An abandoned dairy barn next to a collection of huge concrete tanks and several dilapidated houses brought back the feeling of driving through ghost towns.

Farther ahead, the paved road which passes the turnoff for El Combate (a popular seaside village) becomes a mixture of dirt and sand closer to the lighthouse. A weathered site described on our map as the center of the salt industry sprawls across the spit of land leading to the lighthouse promontory. Salt flats in this area have been industrially mined for their salt since 1511. Shallow crystallizing pools dwarf a shack and windmill-like structure. Mounds of salt glisten like snow around machinery that looks patched beyond serviceability. Yet according to the salt farm's manager, the machinery still functions, and the farm produces thousands of tons of salt yearly for industrial and animal feed use. We met the manager by chance at the nearby Agua al Cuello (water up to the neck) Restaurant, a picturesque place on stilts in the water.

The lighthouse looms at the end of a maze of roads, all in poor condition. This building, part of a system of lighthouses built by the Spanish colonial government a century ago, perhaps best exemplifies the government's interest in placing the lighthouses in areas of dramatic scenery. Two hundred-foot cliffs surround the neo-classical building; in the distance, a mere strip of beach separates a doorknob-shaped bay from an extensive lagoon.

The two wings of the lighthouse were originally two separate but identical living quarters for the keepers and their families. The tower contained the lantern and equipment for maintaining it. The building is no longer inhabited; its windows and doors are cemented shut and graffiti mar its walls. An electric light long ago replaced the manually operated one, but a black weathervane atop the tower still provides the same service it has provided for a hundred years.

Boquerón and beyond

Two extraordinary beaches, maxi and mini in size, developed and undeveloped, are separated by an intriguing area of monolithic limestone formations, a bird-decked lagoon, mangrove forests, legendary caves and an old railroad tunnel. The beaches are Boquerón and Buyé, and the land in between is Punta Guaniquilla.

I once hiked from one beach to the other. Though the hike itself was less than satisfactory (featuring unmarked cow paths, restless cattle, barbed wire, barking dogs, simmering roads), the sites are worth describing.

On the map Boquerón looks as if some celestial alligator has taken a giant bite out of the land, leaving a deeply recessed bay. Along the innermost curve is a bathing resort, a mile-long arc of lifeguarded beach and rental cabins half hidden by palm trees. Joggers, snorkelers, wind surfers and boaters make use of the beach along with less active bathers, loungers and picnickers.

To the south a sprawling lagoon framed by mangroves harbors a sampling of just about every species of water bird in Puerto Rico. From the shores of this bird refuge, we spotted brown pelicans **(pelícano),** green herons **(martinete)** and a royal tern **(gaviota real)** perched on a channel post.

To the north is the **barrio** of Boquerón, a place of fishermen, wooden homes and sandswept streets — officially too small to be given town status, but swollen every weekend with beachgoers who crowd around roadside stands displaying fresh oysters. Along the northern half of the bay a strip of mangrove forest and several salt flats separate the water from denuded hills used for grazing. Weathered troughs lie under rain trees **(samán)**, whose flat pods, relished by cattle, make a rustling rainlike sound in the breezes.

A small handpainted sign directs visitors down a dirt lane to Playa Buyé, where two miniature crescent-shaped beaches aesthetically rival most any place in the Caribbean. The only signs of tourist development the weekday we visited were men collecting a dollar for parking and a lone refreshment van. A dozen houses border half the beach. A nearby brick oven, once used to convert local limestone into lime, is encroached on by grasses.

Visitors lounged on bone-colored sand under shade trees. The water was partly translucent, partly darkened by patches of sea grass and coral. Nautical vehicles ranged from an innertube to a 30-foot motorboat. Two men in a rowboat dubbed "Pulpo" snorkeled the area systematically for octopus and lobster. A man followed by three young boys spearfished in the smaller bay which is fringed at the far side with seaward-tilting palms.

South of the houses at Buyé a jeep trail cuts through dry vegetation to the brick and lime ruins of a house and windmill at the top of a hill. From here there is a splendid view of Bahía de Boquerón and Laguna Guaniquilla. During the wet season (when I visited) the lagoon is filled with water and water birds. In dry weather the water evaporates, exposing cracked, ash-colored soil. Massive limestone shapes loom above the lagoon, serrated monuments formed by water and wind erosion that conjured up prehistoric or extragalactic associations in my mind.

Equally eerie were thousands of beetle-sized crabs, which crawled en masse to aquatic safety as we approached the water's edge. We spotted a number of birds, including smooth-billed ani **(judío)** with long tails

A. *Salt flats near Cabo Rojo lighthouse* B. *House and plaza, San Germán* C. *Cabo Rojo light* D. *Salt wo...*

and hooked beaks, black-necked stilts **(viuda)** and ruddy turnstones **(playero turco)** with their harlequin patterns. Pearly eyed thrashers **(zorzal pardo)** shrilled in the background.

Cofresí, a local pirate executed in 1825, grew up in Guaniquilla and used a group of caves next to the lagoon as a hideout. Stories about the Cofresí caves abound; no two versions are the same. One of the most interesting tells of a nephew of Cofresí who supposedly lived in the house on the hill (one resident denied that relatives of Cofresí ever lived there) and hid the pirate from time to time. After Cofresí's death authorities pestered him about the pirate's "remains" — his booty — until the nephew went into one of the caves and committed suicide. A memorial to him (some say his crypt) at the spot is now defaced, apparently by later treasure seekers. (This seeker did not even find the caves).

The San Juan/Ponce railroad line, which ceased functioning in the mid-1950's, stopped in Boquerón primarily to collect sugar cane, but also to deposit vacationers at the well-known (even then) bathing resort. Shrub-covered cuts in the Guaniquilla hills, railroad beds strewn with leaves and limbs, and an arched tunnel built in 1908 are all that remain. A recess in the narrow tunnel provided safety for people caught unaware by an oncoming train. One nearby resident laughed when reminded of the recess, explaining that she was caught there when a child some 30 years ago and could still remember the reverberating din of the train.

A glimpse of San Germán

San Germán, the second oldest town in Puerto Rico (Caparra/San Juan was first), was founded in 1512 by Diego Columbus and subsequently destroyed numerous times — by pirates, Indians, European rivals and even mosquitoes — forcing its founding fathers to relocate. A century later marked the founding of Porta Coeli. Its recently restored chapel, situated on a knoll at the end of one of San Germán's two plazas, is now a museum containing Mexican colonial religious paintings and 18th - and 19th - century statues. The more ornate but less venerable church of San Germán de Auxerre faces the square town hall in the second plaza. More recently, Inter American University's first campus was built on lovely grounds on the outskirts of town.

We stayed overnight in San Germán at the Oasis Hotel, a restored building surrounding an inner patio which is part of the island's **parador** network of country inns. The downtown area has the same historic feel as Old San Juan, with colonial homes built close together, narrow balconies and old-fashioned street lamps. Only the blue cobblestones and bustle of Old San Juan are missing.

1990s UPDATE: The problems caused by the homes and houseboats, some tied up to mangroves, along La Parguera's coast has increased; as a result, the phosphorescence of its bay and the clarity of its waters have decreased. Help is apparently on the way as Federal agencies begin to enforce laws protecting coastal zones. On more positive ecological notes, the U.S. Fish and Willdlife has set up bird-watching trails and a visitor center (851-7258) on its refuge south of Boquerón and is cleaning up the nearby, bird-rich Laguna Cartagena. There is also a coastal lagoon wildlife refuge off Boquerón beach (see the Karst Country article). The Conservation Trust of Puerto Rico protects Punta Guaniquilla; call first (722-5882) if you want to visit the point. The back-road route to La Parguera is along Road 304, and the one to Cabo Rojo lighthouse is along 304, 305 and 303. Playa Buyé is off Road 307 several miles north of Boquerón. In Parguera, the Shell Mound Museum has closed; ask about the status of the bars and restaurants. In Cabo Rojo, the picturesque Agua al Cuello Restaurant has been torn down. There are now six **paradores** in southwest Puerto Rico; call 721-2884 for details. For information about renting cabins at Boquerón, see the Secret Beach article.

A NOTE ABOUT LIGHTHOUSE IN PUERTO RICO: The Spanish colonial government developed a system of lighthouses in Puerto Rico whose purpose was to improve trade by better illuminating the coasts. The lighthouses, mostly built between 1880 and 1898, were all designed in the same neo-classical style and set in areas of impressive coastal scenery. All are now included in the Federal Register of Historic Places. For the location of the lights, see the center map of **Qué Pasa** magazine. Several of the lighthouses are in ruins; the others have been converted to unmanned, automatic operation and, in most cases, are sealed with concrete to prevent vandalism. The Cabo San Juan lighthouse is now part of the Cabezas de San Juan Nature Reserve (see Fajardo article) and the Punta Tuna lighthouse in Maunabo (see the Southeast Puerto Rico article) will soon be turned over to the Conservation Trust of Puerto Rico. The Arecibo lighthouse (879-1625) has been restored and is now a museum. The U.S. Coast Guard hopes to find good tenants for the other lights; call the Aids to Navigation Office (729-6800) for more information.

Parguera's cays

TRAMPING ON MONA

Isla de Mona, situated halfway between Puerto Rico and the Dominican Republic, is not for people who complain about walking a dozen miles in oven heat and relentless sun; who believe a meal is incomplete without fresh meat or that water is always a tap away; who would weep if they sat on a bed of baby cacti or pellets of goat excrement. Mona is for those willing to accept primitive conditions, a relatively hostile environment and ecological precautions to glimpse an island opulent in natural sculptures, flora and fauna oddities, and historical remains.

Getting ready

"Mona is rough," cautioned René Colón, leader of the Natural History Society's (NHS) four-day visit to Mona, at a pre-trip meeting. His advice included chewing pebbles to avoid thirst, lathering with liquid detergent in oceanic baths and packing to carry everything on our backs. The half dozen vehicles on the island belong to the Department of Natural Resources (DNR), which manages the island, and are not for public use. Perhaps most impressive, we would be lugging five-gallon water jugs. Water, once plentiful, is now limited to a few brackish or contaminated wells. When finished, Colón was almost hidden by a mound of cans, food, packs, jugs and utensils brought to emphasize his points.

Getting there

At midnight one weekend in July, two shrimp boats carrying our Mona expedition moved away from coastal lights into star-specked darkness. Passengers bedded down in nooks. The sea was exceptionally calm for the notorious Mona Passage. Halfway across, the moon and two distant ship lights lit the thick blackness. Some six hours after we left port, the sheer limestone cliffs of Mona's northern coast rose 200 feet from the sea, and pink clouds seemed to ready the sun for its morning ascent.

The boat circled the seven-by-four-mile, lima-bean-shaped island, bobbing past a lighthouse, shrub-topped cliffs pocked with caves, strips of white sand, casuarina trees poking above dry subtropical forest, and finally the dock and glassy water of Playa Sardinera, 50 miles west of

A. *Playa Sardinera, Mona* B. *Brown booby and egg*

Mayagüez. A skiff took passengers and gear to the dock, where the expedition split into two groups. One remained on Playa Sardinera, site of brackish showers and the DNR Vigilante Corps base; the other set off to camp at the more primitive and secluded Playa Uvero.

On the road to Uvero

Mahogany and pine-coned casuarina trees line the start of the four-mile loam-and-stone road to Uvero. Both the trees and the road are products of the Civilian Conservation Corps' stay on Mona in the late 1930's and early 40's. Long prop roots, bromeliads, palms, vines and brittle gray rock highlight the dry forest. At the junction with Mona's turf airport runway, the tall trees seem to wave goodbye. Beyond, the road becomes an inferno.

A mile detour on a palmetto-lined lane leads to Playa Carabinero. Here the sand is garnished with pine needles, sea urchin shells, a large abandoned rowboat and thick piebald hawsers. At the beach, we looked beyond massive coral rocks to a sailboat on the horizon. By watching the boat and letting the imagination go, we could easily envision the time when piracy endangered Mona's waters.

For 300 years until the late 1800's the respectable steered clear of Mona because of frequent invasions by pirates and privateers. French, English, Spanish, even African corsairs battled, sunk, captured and hid in the area, leaving tales of raped women, starved, parched pirates in cave hideouts, and Spanish attacks on North American vessels. James Lancaster, "El Portugués", and Cofresí passed through, and it is conjectured that Captain Kidd stashed booty, possibly 60,000 pounds sterling, on Mona before sailing to the U.S. (and his hanging in 1701). This conjecture has lured many treasure seekers to Mona and produced tales of suicide, insanity, wrecks — and empty pockets.

Easy living

Life slows down at Playa Uvero. Visitors cool off on the rickety porch of an abandoned shack (at a later visit, the shack was razed). The breezes and silence which permeate tents set up under low-lying trees along the beach lull campers into a state of languor. Children cavorting in the sand and water look like butterflies of motion against an impassive sea.

More energetic visitors walk to the nearby Cueva de Doña Geña. The shallow cave is named for Eugenia Rodríguez, who lived in it from 1910 to 1943 with her three sons while working part of the time as a cook for guano miners. One of the sons died on Mona. Another eventually moved to New York City, a stunning change of pace. In the same area remains of stone walls date back to the late 1800's when Carlos Iglesias cleared land and traded products including charcoal, vegetables, plantains and swine until he was poisoned, reportedly by liquor intended for a ship captain.

At night, bright constellations, soft breezes and quiet waves mesmerize campers into sleep.

Rough hiking

The sun was not yet up when we ascended from coastal land to limestone plateau for a hike halfway around the island. The almost cool air at this time of day seems to sharpen images, from the flaking copper-colored bark of gumbo-limbo (**almácigo**) trees and the oily, lemony smells of dusty vegetation to the swoop of an American kestrel (**falcón**) and the coo of a zenaida dove (**tórtola**).

Below the desolate junction of Hell and Lighthouse roads are the guano mining ruins of Cueva Pájaro, as well as a slender beach and the nearly-disappeared cabin of a man named Erickson. In the early 1920's Erickson built the cabin and systematically searched the island for treasure; two years after he arrived, he went insane and had to be hospitalized.

At the junction, two concrete road strips lead to a distant lighthouse. Cacti and twisted trees poke out of miles of unbroken tabletop shrub. An intense sun beats down, adding a surrealistic shimmer to the scene. Goats occasionally appear along the road. Thousands of them now overrun the island and, along with wild pigs, cats, roosters and rats, threaten fragile flora and fauna.

The lighthouse, a large beacon inside a black tower atop a peeling blue and white building, was used by the DNR staff until recently; a higher, automatic light on the other side of Mona has taken over the lighthouse's original function. There is no trail along the northern escarpment, where 200-foot cliffs fall into indigo water. Sounds are rare — clangs, resembling those of loose manhole covers, from jagged rocks underfoot, buzzing wasps, wind — and shade is even rarer. Isolated tangles of fig trees, prop roots and vines jut from narrow sinkholes. Goat droppings and cacti shaped like sea urchins top the rocks. Leafless **alelí** trees cling to the ground. In places, prickly shrubs extend to the very edge of the escarpment.

The most famous of many plant and animal species peculiar to Isla de Mona is the Mona ground iguana, mini-replica of the dinosaur age. We spotted a three-foot specimen sunning on the toothy rock. Its skin resembled dirty mildewed leather, and the legs and throat seemed too small for such baggy skin. The iguana yawned and sneezed, and its heart-shaped head followed us as we photographed it from all sides.

Halfway around the island, some nine miles from Playa Uvero, is a red-footed booby nesting site. Sleek brown young boobies and grayish brown and white adults soar harmoniously against a triangular expanse of sky, sea and plateau. At certain times of the year booby nests are wedged into cracks and cacti branches, and chicks overrun the site. Colonies of white-tailed tropicbirds, magnificent frigate birds and other sea birds also nest on Mona and the smaller adjacent Isla de Monito.

The northern coast is so barren and the air was so hot that when the lighthouse once again poked out of the landscape on our return trip, it seemed a mirage.

A magical cave

The toothy, algae-covered entrance to Cueva Lirio lies half-hidden just east of the lighthouse. Beyond its mouth, narrowing rooms showcase marvelous beige stalactite and stalagmite formations, including calcite maidens, mushrooms and sheep dogs. The basin of one pool rimmed with scalloped calcite is covered with what seem to be filigreed blossoms. When flashlights are turned off, the blackness of the cave seems to glow, and the silence to throb.

We scrawled arrows in the sand to prevent getting lost and embarked on a magical hour's walk through the cave. Several natural windows frame cliff and sea. The main tunnel opens into a museum-like nave with sinkhole skylights and an eons-old rock "exhibit" of mammals, bisons and giant eggs that would have pleased Rodin.

Old beams, tramway tracks and rusted cable-car skeletons in the next room allude to the years, from 1848 to 1927, when mining removed some 160,000 metric tons of guano from Mona caves. Guano, decomposed bat manure mixed with limestone detritus, contains phosphates, which make it useful as fertilizer. On Mona, guano was shoveled into cable cars, pulled to cliff windows and lowered into ships. Mining was no easy task: ships were lost in the rough seas and worker turnover was high, due to the sauna conditions of the caves. One dedicated mining manager is said to have lived inside Cueva Lirio.

Raised cable tracks connect rooms festooned with drippings and calcite-rimmed pools, totem columns and ornate ice-like sheets. Where the tracks end, a ladder leans against a sinkhole which provides an exit from the cave. A grassy trail leads back to Lighthouse Road.

***

We journeyed back to Playa Uvero at night. Land crabs surprised by flashlights seemed to scuttle faster than the passing hikers. Pearly-eyed thrashers **(zorzal pardo)**, the most common land birds on Mona, chirped encouragement. Shelled hermit crabs watched from the sidelines. At certain phases of the moon, thousands of these crabs migrate to beaches to spawn. Below us, limestone caps dolomite rock; both are derived from ancient marine deposits. Equally intriguing, perhaps Christopher Columbus or Ponce de León once explored this very route. Perhaps, but we were then too tired to care.

Historical and natural resources

Set in the cliffs behind Playa Sardinera is another cave, Cueva Negra, known to have contained pictographs and petroglyphs etched on its soft limestone surface by Taino Indians. Tainos inhabited Mona, reportedly calling it Amoná and using it as a link in their Caribbean canoeing journeys, possibly up to 2,000 years before Columbus' arrival on Mona in 1494.

The Indians raised **yuca** for cassava (some roots were too big for one man to carry...), oranges, vegetables and wild cotton from which they made shirts for Ponce de León's troops. They lived in communal **bohíos** housing up to 50 people and remained on Mona until 1578, when the few survivors of pirate raids were transported to Puerto Rico. All that remains today are potsherds, drawings and the ruins of two ceremonial ball courts (a faint trail near Playa Uvero leads to one of them).

Also in Sardinera is a small colonial jail built into rocks and the leaky Cueva del Agua, where we discovered writing dating to the early 1970's...

Several hundred feet from the caves' prehistoric darkness, iridescent tropical fish swim around some of the best coral in Puerto Rico near a beach set at the foot of a cliff. Underwater horizontal visibility on Mona reaches 200 feet. Ornate slabs of staghorn coral, as well as sea fans, finger coral and massive brain coral frame schools of fish that include paper-thin blue tang and silvery grunts. The sea is rich with a variety of marine animals, from red snapper and rock lobster to whales and hawksbill turtles, which commonly nest on Mona beaches. Flotsam from as far as the Amazon and Africa has washed up here.

Our last night was spent at Playa Sardinera, more popular with visitors than Playa Uvero. We spotted a "dead man walking," a night heron **(yaboa)** whose upright walk sounds uncannily human. There were also many live men reveling at other tentsites, a scene reminiscent of the old pirate days. We pondered the effect of so much human activity on the island's fragile wildlife.

In the morning we mimicked the hermit crabs as we migrated en masse to the dock and boats. Flying phenomena entertained us on the return ride. There were flying fish which glided over the water, flying birds, flying waves which caused flying stomachs--and flying spirits now acquainted with Mona island.

A. *Mona lighthouse* B. *Mona ground iguana*

Mona's northern cliffs

1900s UPDATE: Mona continues to be a nature refuge, accessible only by charter plane or boat. Choose your boat and captain well, for the Mona Passage can get very rough. Camping is primitive: everything, including water, must be brought in, and everything, including garbage, must be taken out. Regulated hunting is permitted. Call the Department of Natural Resources (724-3724) for the required camping permits and more information.

A NOTE ABOUT NHS AND OTHER GROUPS: The Natural History Society (NHS) promotes the study and appreciation of natural history and encourages conservation of Puerto Rico's natural resources. There are monthly meetings, field trips, and camping expeditions. Mona visits, extremely popular, are exclusively for members. For more information write: NHS, PO Box 361036, San Juan PR 00936-1036. The San Juan based Fondo de Mejoramiento conducts innovative islandwide tours emphasizing culture, history, the environment, and periodic visits to Mona. Call 759-8366 for more information. Similar groups are located in Ponce (Turisla de Puerto Rico, 843-6972) and Mayagüez (Conozcamos a Puerto Rico, 831-0865). An increasing number of nature/adventure tour operators are offering outings to such places as Mona; see **Qué Pasa** for a partial listing.

A. *Punta Higüero lighthouse, Rincón* B. *Surfer*

RINCON IN WINTER

Rincón, a hilly town on the island's western tip, is well endowed with mango trees and rural charm. Its uncrowded beaches seem made for postcards. Its sea lures bathers, surfers — and humpback whales. Even when viewed through drizzles and downpours, as I did, the town's attributes shine through.

***

That weekend, one of the wettest on record, was a reminder that tropical islands are still at the whim of nature, in spite of man's attempts to harness it. On the way to Rincón, what we had hoped to be merely a cloudburst extended across the entire island. White sky and rain pelting on the road in front of us resembled a blizzard; on either side hills looked like the steamy Amazon. Highway 2, known for its strings of traffic jams, junkyards and urbanizations, became a route of large puddles and small lakes which eventually rendered the road impassable, but not before we slipped through.

On the outskirts of town

A road bordered with houses and mango trees ascends from Rincón toward 1,188-foot Pico Atalaya, which means "lookout peak" in Spanish. Grazing pastures cover pointed hills. At the top, a weathered, hatted man standing next to several houses perched on the slope nodded good day. With little prodding, he expounded on the whereabouts of his 18 children and 53 grandchildren: most have built on this property, while some have settled in New York.

The views from the antenna-topped peak resemble three-dimensional Viewmaster frames. To the south the mountains descend almost vertically to a valley of square sugar cane fields. The palm-fringed Playa Añasco public bathing resort, the Río Grande de Añasco delta and Mayagüez edge a large bay. Somewhere in this area — possibly at Río Añasco — Taino Indians accompanied Antonio Salcedo across a river in 1509 and proceeded to drown him, apparently to test whether or not Spaniards were mortal. To the north, coned hills extend to the tip of Puerto Rico, and a valley fans toward Aguadilla.

A. *View south from Pico Atalaya* B. *Rincón street and Buena Vida Surf Shop*

On the southern side of Pico Atalaya the road plunges down toward Centro Calvache and the ocean, past streams and lush vegetation, scarlet poinsettia and magenta bougainvillaea, several abandoned homes and patches of wild sugar cane. A wall between the sea and the road is a remnant of the route of the old railroad that once circled much of the island. Australian pines, a peeling boat and fishermen's lockers surround the Capilla de Carmen. This concrete chapel, containing benches, a miniature wooden boat and plastic flowers next to ceramic religious figures, is dedicated to Carmen, patron saint of the fishermen.

Closer to town, walls partly hidden under flowering vegetation characterize the Villa Cofresí Hotel, named for the legendary pirate, and the Villa Antonio Beach Resort. That day a Christmas tree stood in the Cofresí lobby and a lone sunbather lay on a long expanse of beach under a cloudy sky.

Saturday night in Rincón

Our first stop that night was La Bohemia Restaurant/Bar on the seacoast of Punta Higüero, one hill and a steep grade beyond Rincón. Palm trunks held up the zinc roofed, plexiglass-enclosed structure. The conviviality around its bar and pool table contrasted with the thick rural darkness. A constant easterly wind bent coconut trees in an adjacent field. Waves lapped several yards from the bar. Far to the east specks of light from Aguadilla glittered and beckoned. On a subsequent visit, the place had closed.

On the other side of the hill the Black Eagle Restaurant is cloaked in the same nighttime darkness. Scattered about its three large dining areas are resin-coated spool tables, a juke box and craft items for sale. A variety of crafts — palm frond baskets and hats, shell jewelry and candles, clothes and shawls, coconut-headed decanter figures and blowfish lamps, even surfboards and sailboards – are made and sold in Rincón.

While sipping drinks, we learned of other options for Saturday night entertainment (Friday's magnet is the Mayagüez Mall). They include stopping at El Faro or Rancho Uno Bar, or attending the occasional dances at the nuclear reactor building, once a cafeteria for the Bonus Thermonuclear Energy Plant, now used by local groups for social functions.

Sunday morning in Rincón

In 1776 Friar Iñigo Abbad, first to write a history of Puerto Rico, described Santa Rosa del Rincón, founded in 1772, as having 11 houses, one church, 210 families and 1,130 souls in the surrounding hills. Cattle and fruit trees thrived in the valleys, and rice and tobacco were cultivated. The small town could not defend itself against marauding privateers.

In 1878 Rincón, which depended on Aguada in military and judicial matters, consisted of five streets, a "highway" and an alley. The first purely civil marriage in Puerto Rico took place here in 1894. While in operation, the Córcega sugar mill produced 12,000 sacks of sugar annually.

A. *Lookout at Punta Borinquen* B. *Surfer near Punta Higüero*

Today there are some 1,550 inhabitants in the town and 10,000 in the municipality. Its plaza now has only one tree: a second was cut down when the new bandshell was constructed, and current legend has it that a third was removed after someone climbed the tree in inebriated enthusiasm and fell.

Cars filled the streets as Rinconians attended Sunday services in two churches at opposite ends of the plaza. Many wooden buildings frame the square. Two pharmacies, a bakery and a bar were open. A man greeted church members as they left mass. Two men ogling women sat on a stoop beside the bar. Three lithe, tanned youths with sun-bleached hair left the bakery. At the end of one street, past the church and homes with shutter doors and Spanish balconies, sat "Mean Gene" Crunkleton's Buena Vida Surf Shop, now closed.

Of surf, surfing and surfers

In 1968 Rincón hosted the World Surfing Championship. Before that, handfuls of mostly North American surfers had ventured to Puerto Rico's western tip in search of waves, and were well rewarded. Since the championship, the town's population has swelled in winter months when hundreds of surfing enthusiasts (fewer in recent years) break from jobs or studies to rent rooms and spend days scouting the best surf. Numbers swell even more on weekends with followers from the San Juan area and intrigued local youth.

Duke Michael, one of Rincón's pioneer surfers and a long-time town resident, toured the surfing beaches with me. Behind the Black Eagle Restaurant is Little Malibu Beach, named for similar, larger waves in Malibu, California. Coconut palms fringe the sand around a new marina. The surf must be high to produce waves worth riding at this beach: to the south, the sea becomes docile, suitable for bathing; to the north, waves increase in size.

Rincón surfers, like their California counterparts, have given simple names to their favorite surf breaks, such as "Steps," "Marías," and "Domes." A slick path off the road to the north leads to Steps, named for concrete steps which surrealistically poke out of the sand. Outside the break is a second set of waves, called Tres Palmas for the three palms surfers fix on when in the water. That day Steps had the best surfing. Cars lined the road, and two dozen men sat on boards seesawing over waves. A wave swelled, one surfer began to paddle, the wave arched and he stood up, shooting forward yet somehow glued to the board, balanced between sea and sky. Suddenly he flipped over the top of the wave and paddled out for another ride. Underwater reef here and at most Rincón beaches makes them dangerous for novice surfers.

María's, farther north, was named in memory of a woman who had lived by the beach and been kind to early surfers. The Beach House Surf Shop is here, run by a man who first visited Rincón 15 years ago and eventually gave up his job in Chicago to surf and sell surfing paraphernalia.

Beyond a candle-shaped lighthouse is Domes, probably the most popular surfing beach, named for a huge nuclear reactor dome nearby. The Bonus Thermonuclear Energy Plant opened here as a demonstration model of an advanced nuclear reactor design in 1964, but ceased functioning in the early 1970's. Now the beach is a recreational area, with makeshift picnic facilities. Several teenagers were riding wavelets on squat boogie boards.

In Punta Higüero an increase in the number of houses and house additions reflects the influence of surfing on this community in the last decade. Although surfing was initially criticized as a sport of drug abusers and hippies, Michael feels that now the relationship between surfers and the local community is harmonious for the most part, and that residents are recognizing the serious, skilled aspects of the sport.

Pool and Sandy Beach are surfing sites in Punta Higüero; farther to the north are Table Rock Beach and Wilderness at Punta Borinquen, where the waves are generally two to three feet higher than in Rincón. At the bottom of the hill is the Punta Higüeras Resort and at the top is Kahuna's Guest House, two classic stops for visiting surfers.

What makes people like Duke Michael drop out of lives of material or intellectual success in favor of the surfing lifestyle? Michael mentioned the adventure of traveling to different places, the satisfaction of mastering a skill after many years of practice, the "high" felt when skimming gracefully in front of a fine wave, the surprise of childhood friends — eyes lined with dark rings, stomachs protruding — when they see him in the same condition as 20 years ago. And something else, something he just could not explain.

Whales also like Rincón

Beginning in late December every year, humpback whales stop ingesting fish at the Stellwagon Banks off Massachusetts and begin their solitary migrations to warm Caribbean waters. Here they fast, living off accumulated blubber, and mingle socially with whales from other feeding grounds (such as Newfoundland). A single male swims alone, singing a highly complex melody which alternately resembles hiccups, squeaking doors, revving motors, elephants and birds. Suddenly a female sidles up to him, apparently pleased with his rendition, and they wander around the islands together for a few days, presumably mating as they go, then separate and travel, alone again, back north beginning in mid-March. The impregnated female swims south the next year to give birth. Newborn calves are 10 to 15 feet long, weigh some 2,000 pounds, suckle up to 100 gallons of milk daily, return with the mother to her feeding grounds and begin to sing (or listen) within five to seven years.

Each year a large number of these whales are sighted off Rincón's shores, heading east and west. Gauze-white puffs of water snorted from blowholes form and dissolve over the ocean, then glistening black mounds rise, hover above the water for several seconds and sink again. The humpbacks are watched with great interest, for they have been declared an endangered species, made so by the demand for their oil for products ranging from shoe polish to transmission fluid to cosmetics. Rough estimates place eight to ten thousand in the world and two to four thousand in the western North Atlantic.

Several years ago David Mattila came to Rincón with his own sailboat, his own money and some support from the World Wildlife Fund to track humpback whales on their winter sojourn south. Each winter he has returned, recently with more extensive funding and additional whale watchers, to rise before six every morning and motor along the coast in search of whales. The group plots whale sightings, records whale songs and photographs the acrobatic humpbacks as they breach (jump) or flip their tails. Each fluke (tail) is a unique combination of piebald pigmentation; photographs of flukes can identify individual whales and thus help unravel who's who in migratory routes. These studies have documented that separate northern populations mix in the tropics, remain on the move (except for singers, mothers and calves) and breed off Puerto Rico. Though not yet documented, the large number of calves sighted off the island's northwest tip indicates it is a major calving ground.

A last meal

The Black Eagle Restaurant was named for the owner's father-in-law, who would imitate that bird when it was necessary to leave card games quickly. Here we tried several of the restaurant's renowned specialties, which include steaks and freshly caught seafood. Ten miles out to sea the island of Desecheo formed a bulky shadow through the continuing rain. Several Rincón residents discussed tourism, expressing a mixture of relief and puzzlement that more people have not discovered the town and its beaches. We were puzzled, too.

Sunset from the Black Eagle

Surfer, Desecheo island in background

1900s UPDATE: In 1988 the World Surfing Championship were again held in northwest Puerto Rico, reaffirming the region's excellent surfing conditions. Villa Antonio Beach Resort (823-2645) has become a **parador**, and the elegant, expensive, away-from-it-all Hornet Dorset Primavera Hotel (823-4030, no children allowed) opened a couple of years ago to excellent reviews. Pico Atalaya is reached by roads 412 and 411, but the peak itself is on private property. Capilla de Carmen is south of Playa Córcega on Road 429. Road 413 north passes the Black Eagle Restaurant, several surfing beaches and Punta Higüero. Ask about shops and surfing guesthouses. Several boats now offer whale watching from January through March; harassing the whales in any way is a Federal offense.

A NOTE ABOUT SURFING: Although Rincón is the island's best known surfing area, there are also excellent beaches north of Rincón to Punta Borinquen and around the coast to Jobos near Isabela. Surfers also head to Stops Five and Eight in Puerta de Tierra, Pine Grove in Isla Verde, Aviones in Piñones east of San Juan and Los Tubos in Manatí. A surfshop or two in Rincón may rent surfing equipment, but most water sports centers rent only windsurfers.

ON THE TRACK OF HISTORY

One day in August 1936, at 8:45 p.m., Gonzalo Córdova boarded a passenger train near Stop 20 in Santurce for an eight-hour ride to his college in Mayagüez. At 1:00 a.m. the train passed Camuy.

One day in August 1981, at 8:45 a.m., the "Official" Trans-Puerto Rico Walking Team, known but to few for treks from Arecibo to Ponce and from Mayagüez to Maunabo along the Ruta Panorámica, began a hike which followed the remains of the old railroad tracks and ended at the foot of another defunct institution, Ramey Air Force Base, (now known as Punta Borinquen), passing several diverse and rugged beaches along the way.

The walking team — dressed in jogging shorts, T-shirts, sneakers and visors, carrying day packs and water bottles — met at a beach halfway between Camuy and Quebradillas. A stone hut on this beach was reportedly once used in contraband slave trade. That morning we were more concerned with a scroll of topographical maps, cut and pasted together and marking our route, than with the panorama of rock, sea and pelicans around us. By the end of the day, however, our interest in history gave way to an appreciation of the northwest coast's natural beauty.

History

In 1888 the Spanish Crown approved a franchise to construct a railroad around Puerto Rico. The line, which was not to exceed speeds of nine miles an hour, was inaugurated in 1907. It connected San Juan, Mayagüez and Ponce with a service for mail, passengers and merchandise.

In 1910 the American Railroad Company bought the San Juan to Ponce line. By 1946 some 420 miles of railroad, owned by several companies, were being used primarily for sugar cane transport. The arrival of motor vehicles started the decline of the train system. A strike over wages, eventually won by the employees, impelled the American Railroad Company to liquidate its assets and transfer ownership of the railroad to the employees. Soon afterward, in the mid-1950's, the railroad ceased functioning.

***

Railroad bridge near Quebradillas

A farmer carrying a milk bucket stared at the string of hikers as we started out on a wide path through pastureland. A cow seemed to chew thoughtfully as it watched us. At first, imagination was needed to envision trains traveling along this abandoned, overgrown roadbed, now bare of ties and rails. Impressive cuts through limestone hills provided the first obvious clues that we were on the right track.

The route, lost in a bulldozed field, reappears at a 60-foot-high concrete viaduct completed in 1922 which once carried the narrow-gauge trains across a gorge. From this vantage point passengers could survey hills covered with dusty legume trees, **alelí** and seagrapes as well as limestone cliffs dropping 150 feet to the ocean. Now the bridge and gorge form the boundary of a park, part of Campo del Caballo, the island's first Arabian horse farm.

A paved road which buries the railroad bed leads past a coconut-headed scarecrow (on a second visit the scarecrow had acquired a wife and child) and several **colmados** to the Guajataca lookout. A picnic area here enables visitors to combine lunch with one of the most impressive views in Puerto Rico. Hills descend into the Río Guajataca valley, waves file into a bay and break near a beach overlooked by a modern **parador,** and El Tunel pokes a hole through the far hills. This arched railroad tunnel, notoriously narrow in its day, opens onto a roadbed set between a cliff and a wall that separates it from waves crashing on rocks. We reflected on the thrill passengers must have felt traveling through this section.

Reflections

In 1919 travel writer Harry A. Franck decided to see the Puerto Rican countryside by train. He remarked on the cleanliness and conveniences of the cars — ice water, paper cups, blotter roll towels. First class, with comfortable cushioned swivel chairs, cost three cents per kilometer; hard wooden benches in second class cost two and one-quarter cents. Diagonally placed bunk bed cabins in the rear sleeping car had individual toilet facilities, thermos bottles of water and electric lights. According to Franck, the train's only fault was an annoying tendency to stop at the next station while only barely underway from the previous one.

In the 1930's Gonzalo Córdova traveled by train while a student at Mayagüez Agriculture College. He, too, speaks of the trains taking "forever" and stopping "everywhere," although they were cheaper than buses. The San Juan to Ponce line started at a landmark tower station (now demolished) in Old San Juan. Córdova boarded at the next stop, paying first-class fare for the all-night ride. Usually one of the half dozen cars was for mail and baggage. The cars curved around the city, making full stops and flag stops (where passengers had to flag the train to stop) before rolling along the coast.

There was no restaurant car, so at every stop passengers dashed out to buy snacks from station vendors. Each town developed a reputation for certain foods that generally still holds. Bayamón sold crisp pork rinds

(chicharrones) while Dorado provided fried codfish **(bacalao frito).** Arecibo was known for fishcakes of **cetí,** a tiny fish which swims in schools and places its eggs in the Río Arecibo. Quebradillas sold tropical fish (for pets, not food), and Isabela's specialty was rich leaf cheese **(queso de hoja).** The Aguadilla station, halfway to Ponce, had a restaurant specializing in marinated fish **(escabeche).** All Córdova remembers about the Mayagüez station, where he arrived at 4:00 a.m., is its coffee. Had he continued, he could have sampled pudding in San Germán, biscuits **(galletas)** in Yauco and **quenepa** fruits in Ponce.

***

Beyond the Guajataca tunnel, the railroad bed is half hidden under weeds and low-hanging branches. Below is a coastal scene of boulders, shrubs, dunes and fenced fields. Shortleaf fig **(jagüey blanco)** trees drape roots down small manmade canyons.

We were soon crouching under and maneuvering over numerous barbed wire fences in order to remain on the track. (The fences enable rotation of cattle grazing pastures). A resident pointed out that this is now private ranch land; bilingual private property signs emphasize the point. By this time we had developed a fondness for the track, and somewhat nostalgically took a last look at it extending in the distance, criss-crossed by fences, before we detoured onto a road.

Nostalgia

Soon after the opening of the railroad, José D. Caro, 11 years old at the time, became an assistant to the station manager in Rincón. From 1921 to 1949 he managed the Martin Peña station in San Juan. His son, Salvador Caro, remembers railroad life.

"When Puerto Rico was an agricultural island," Caro said, "products were moved by the trains. Oh, they were slow, never exceeding 25 miles an hour, and powered by coal until the late '40 s, but they were cheaper and more available than trucks at that time. During the harvesting season, special trains moved cane to the sugar mills. Closed cars carried molasses and cargo across the island. Grapefruits were shipped in crates, mangoes in sacks from Rincón and other towns. Aguadilla cotton was sold near the Martin Peña station. Horses were shipped to the old Ponce racetrack by train.

"At times the tracks got slippery in places of high humidity, and men had to throw sand on them to keep the trains from skidding. But they arrived, with mail and water for neighborhoods that had no wells. Residents lined up with five-gallon jugs for the water, which was provided free of charge. No, the trains couldn't compete with motor vehicles and roads built after World War II, and now most of the railroad rights of way have been sold or rented. But the trains served Puerto Rico well during some very bad times for close to half a century."

History gives way to northwest coast beaches

Several back roads lead from the tracks to the Punta Sardina beach near Isabela. On the way we spoke to a farmer who, when queried, reminisced about how he used to wave to the trains from his house. His neighbors whispered as we passed by; a toothless man touched his hat in greeting.

Palms permanently bent to leeward border a dirt road which zigzags down to Punta Sardina. Rocks in the ocean receive the brunt of the waves, especially strong in winter, and shelter a natural pool. Cemented sand dune rocks "tongue" into the sea. Rental cabins and the many bathers attested to the beach's local popularity.

Beyond this point, in spite of swollen feet and bodies sauteed by the sun, the hike became a pleasant amble along partly dirt, partly asphalt roads paralleling the ocean. Magnificent frigate birds flew over the carcass of an abandoned L-shaped hotel, overgrown with palms. Several spirited horses eluded their herder in a field between karst hills and the sea. Along the shoreline, seagrapes poke out of sand dunes and patches of sea lavender **(tobaco marino)** grow on top of jagged rocks. These rocks were also sand dunes at one time; over the eons they became cemented together. Waves splash over the rocks and wind blows sand across the dunes.

Jeeps, Volkswagens and bicycles, all festooned with surfboards, overtook us on the road. We discovered their destination when we arrived at Punta Jacinto, also known as Jobos beach, famous for its good surfing. Two cafeterias, blaring **salsa** music at the time, sell drinks and snacks. In the distance beachgoers stood on a rocky carapace-shaped rock in the sea, watching others propel through waves on surfboards. A blowhole in the rock opens onto a churning cauldron of waves hitting against the wall. Next to the hole is an ominous inscription — Corn Dog, 1957-1982.

Continuing westward on a paved road we reached a third beach. Like most local landmarks, it bears several names including Bajura and The Shacks and is not identified by road signs. Brightly painted shacks descend next to a small lagoon to the beach. Dozens of anis were perched in trees around the lagoon. This is said to be one of the best places for snorkeling on the island, when the water is not rough and the current not too strong. Coral extends in a semi-circle from the beach, and there are underwater caves. Windsurfing and scuba diving are also popular here.

One nice way to end the hike would have been at the popular Sea View Wonder Restaurant on the top of the hill, but we continued to Punta Agujereado, some eight miles beyond the start of our beach walk at Isabela. On one side of the wide beach jungly cliffs ascend to the old Ramey Base which is now known as Punta Borinquen and provides housing for island residents and rentals for visitors. On the other side rock slabs held pools of water from a previous high tide. The sea glistened and shadows lengthened as the sun lowered to the horizon.

A. *Tunnel view of Guajataca beach* B. *Railroad tunnel, Guajataca* C. *Steam locomotive for transporting cane (photo by Ricardo Class).*

A. *Roadside scarecrow near Quebradillas* B. *Stone hut and beach between Camuy and Quebradillas*

1900s UPDATE: Although our hike began near the end of Road 4485, site of the stone hut (walk to the riverbed to see it), the most impressive and accessible stretch of the railroad tracks is seen by entering the Guajataca tunnel (Highway 2, km. 103.8, immediately beyond the **parador**) and walking west. The bridge is at the end of Road 485R, east of Guajataca's **area recreativa**. The Campo de Caballo has closed, but worth visiting is nearby Panadería Los Cocos (Road 484), where bread is still baked in a wood-burning oven. Hiking is nice from Punta Sardina west along Road 466 and from the shacks off Road 466R along the beach to the foot of Punta Agujereado at Punta Borinquen. Guajataca has two **paradores**, located back to back, and Punta Borinquen has one; call 721-2884. There are also cabins near Isabela (Villas del Mar Hau, 872-2045). The Sea View Wonder Restaurant has closed. Check **Qué Pasa** or other local tourism magazines for current information about water sports centers, restaurants and other accommodations.

A NOTE ABOUT SAFEGUARDING CARS AND VALUABLES: Many of the backroads on this trip and others in the book are dirt and/or badly weathered. Drivers may prefer to leave their cars by the paved roads and walk, but this merits a caution. Both visitors and locals warn against leaving valuables in cars, and leaving cars unprotected in remote areas, especially along the coast. Take precautions — paradisiacal settings have robberies, too.

A. *Haystack hill, Río Abajo Forest* B. *Observation tower, Guajataca Forest*

JOURNEYS THROUGH
KARST COUNTRY

Although Puerto Rico has one of the highest population densities in the world, there are still rugged and remote places on the island. One such area is the karst country, world-renowned topography characterized by haystack-shaped hills and conical sinkholes, between Manatí and Isabela. Few roads penetrate its thick forests and mazes of hills. Not many visitors pass the occasional wooden houses hugging limestone slopes. Little noise reaches the grazing fields and small farm plots in the valleys. Trails in various states of repair meander through the three forest reserves in this area. Hikers, if not careful, will learn that karst country is still wild and isolated enough for them to get desoriented or even lost. I, for one, discovered this the hard way.

Guajataca Forest Reserve —
by way of the back roads

Back roads leading to the southern entrance of the Guajataca Reserve, farthest west of the karst forests, pass through picturesque country scenes. Grassy fields surround overgrown mounds of limestone rock. Scarlet African tulip tree blossoms add splashes of color to the dusty vegetation. A rusted smokestack rises above a building of corrugated metal, the abandoned remains of the Soller sugar mill. There are still patches of cane, but most of the land is now pasture with many of the narrow-gauge rails from old cane railroads serving as fence posts.

The road skirts Lago Guajataca, a three-mile-long body of water resembling a centipede on the map. Though it seems as if the lake has always fingered into the surrounding hills, it actually rose up in 1934, when the Río Guajataca was dammed for local irrigation. Large-mouth bass and other fish attract fishermen to Guajataca. Periodic tournaments here create tableaux of dangling poles and hatted men in motorboats on the water. Birds and waterfowl, including grebes, reside along the lake. During the summer Boy Scouts vacation on wooded grounds next to the lake at Camp Guajataka and enjoy swimming, hiking, canoeing and bird watching among other activities.

Beyond the lake the road narrows as the hills press closer together, obscuring the direct sunlight. A weathered sign tacked to a boulder announces the reserve. The road soon becomes so narrow that when we passed another car, it almost scraped a cliff and ours almost tilted into a forested sinkhole. Several picnic areas are set off the road, in the few places where there is room to park.

Vine-draped ledges, Río Tanamá

The trails of Guajataca

In contrast to the overgrown, unmarked trails often found in the island's forest reserves, Guajataca boasts 25 miles of well-maintained trails and a map of the trail system, usually available at the ranger station. One of its longest trails, Caballa, connects the reserve with Lago Guajataca. Abundant signs mark most routes. In some places three signs in three stages of weathering identify one trail, and at one intersection we counted eight. Sign names sometimes disagree with map names, but for us part of the fun was guessing where we were and which path to try next. All slope gradually as they ascend and descend the hilly terrain. None seemed to have other hikers the day we were there.

Trail No. 1 leads to an observation tower, a 15-minute walk away. The path is bordered by brittle rock and covered by leaves which crackle underfoot. Classical karst landscape encircles the tower, a covered wooden platform.

The surrounding land looks as if some Great Hand stuck a thumb repeatedly into soft soil to produce sinkholes, mounded higher clumps of land to form haystack hills, then inserted trees, ferns and dangling roots everywhere. Puerto Rico has some of the finest examples of tropical karst in the world. The bizarre topography was caused by the effects of weather on the limestone common to this area. Eons ago, rainwater dissolved the very porous limestone, forming holes which eventually became caves and subterranean rivers. The rivers enlarged the caves until their roofs collapsed to form sinkholes **(abras)**, leaving the remaining cave walls as mounded hills **(mogotes).**

One of the trails skirts precipitous hills and eroding rock walls as it spirals into an extended sinkhole some 500 feet wide and 100 feet deep. Tongues of sanseveria plants and snakelike vines which seem to crawl out of bushes highlight the forest floor. Tree roots have split open numerous rocks, and ferns grow in the cracks. Near the bottom of the sinkhole the ground becomes muddy and the air quite muggy. Vegetation here is denser and greener than at the top, and trees stretch for the sun. There are several small caves in the area. One is said to be a veritable bat nursery.

At the bottom we noticed several plants and trees planted some time ago by a neighboring farmer. Later I looked up the origins of these crops. Bananas, like coconuts, were introduced to Puerto Rico in the 1500's. The floppy leafed **yautia** is native to tropical America and one of its oldest cultivated crops. Breadfruit trees were brought to the West Indies in the late 1700's from Tahiti to provide cheap slave food. Both sweet and sour oranges have grown semi-wild in Puerto Rican mountains for centuries. Grapefruit is thought to have originated in the West Indies through a mutation or hybrid.

As one trail ascends out of the valley, three signs point toward an overgrown path called J. Pérez leading into dense woods. We checked our map; there was no J. Pérez trail. The scene felt like a Twilight Zone rerun. We decided to stay on the main route.

A. *Arecibo Observatory and surrounding karst (photo by Garred Giles)* B. *Local fungi* C. *Gorge of the R Tanamá*

A note about Cambalache Forest Reserve

Landowners interested in foresting their property know Cambalache Forest Reserve east of Arecibo for its nursery **(vivero),** where eucalyptus, mahoe and other lumber tree seedlings are given away during the week. Forest Service personnel think of Cambalache as the place where posts are treated, using a hot and cold bath technique to preserve the wood against decay and termites. Botanists are interested in, among other trees, the large plantations of teak, and ornithologists in the forest's many resident birds. Young children remember it as the picnic site that has seesaws. And hikers like Cambalache for its miles of dirt roads and overgrown jeep lanes that wind through the forest.

Although the terrain in Cambalache is not as dramatic as the other karst forest reserves, it offers some of the most satisfying and easy hiking. The roads, somewhat bumpy due to the limestone, are nevertheless level and wide enough to permit hikers to walk abreast and talk. Foliage shades the routes most of the way. Outside noises do not penetrate the forested hills; only leaves rustling overhead or snapping underfoot and birds disturb the quiet. Few trails are marked, but all are easy to follow. Bend after bend in the roads lure visitors ever deeper into the woods.

Río Abajo Forest Reserve

Road 10, wedged between tall cliffs and the Arecibo river valley, approaches the Río Abajo Forest Reserve south of Arecibo. On the way it passes a cave high in the cliffs across from Los Chorros Restaurant. A stream pours from the cave mouth. One of several caves in the reserve, Los Chorros is the only one easily seen by visitors. A side road leading to the forest curves into a bird's-eye view of Lago Dos Bocas. Below a triangular hill the lake divides into two gaunt fingers. Launches regularly transport area residents across the manmade lake to the road; visitors may also ride the low wooden boats.

First impressions inside the forest are of shade, slender teak trees and mottled rocks. Soon the hills recede from the road, exposing views of karst, here resembling lunar terrain topped with Amazon vegetation. An 80-inch annual rainfall accounts for the dense clutter of plants and trees. Numerous species of native trees, including balsa **(guano)** and trumpet trees **(yagrumo),** share the forest with teak, mahogany and other introduced species. An exodus of Río Abajo farmers in the 1940's in search of better opportunities (steep limestone hills do not make for profitable farming) aided in the regeneration of the forest. Along one road thick bundles of bamboo spread into cathedral arches against a backdrop of wispy blue Australian pines.

Common frogs, wasps and mosquitoes coexist with non-poisonous snakes and more than 30 bird species. There are plans to breed the endangered Puerto Rican parrot (now restricted to the Caribbean National Forest in Luquillo) in Río Abajo, where it was once common.

131

A. *Lago Guajataca* B. *Soller sugar mill* C. *Launches, Lago Dos Bocas*

There are some fears, however, that the construction of a proposed highway through the edge of the reserve could disturb the habitat.

A picnic and camping area near the entrance of the forest contains shelters, tables, barbecues, toilets and running water. Concrete pools built into a stream along the road are no longer used, due to contaminated water. Forest paths lead to views from the top of a hill. Next to the ranger station a sawmill operates as part of a timber management program to make the forest economically viable as well as ecologically vital and aesthetically delightful. Two camps in the reserve which were once used to train Peace Corps volunteers now house forest research and management personnel and a bilingual school.

The road passes a second picnic area, grassy sinkholes and cliffs dangling root streamers before it stops. Beyond is a system of trails that are unmarked and rarely used. We had read that one of them leads to the Río Tanamá, a river canyon with 300-foot walls, land bridges and sinkholes. This alluring description persuaded us to strike out for the river.

Lost in the woods

A lumber road goes by pastures and an abandoned shack before dwindling into a path which is well defined on rocky slopes but overgrown in level stretches. Soon there is only forest in all directions and an occasional limestone outcrop.

We heard the muffled flow of water over rocks and assumed it to be the distant Tanamá. But after the trail skirted a small stream and angled around steep hills, the sound of water faded, then stopped. By 5:00 p.m. we admitted defeat in our search for the river and turned around. Instead of ascending as it "should" have, the trail descended. Here were unfamiliar plant species and a cliff marked with red graffiti.

A sudden downpour drenched our clothes, and our spirits. We retraced steps, carefully followed the trail, but once again found ourselves next to the red graffiti cliff. Shadows darkened the forest. In our nervousness we were convinced that all trails led to the same place, and we sprinted along this descending one. A black Puerto Rican boa circled a tree with mesmerizing fluidity. The path narrowed into a valley of ferns that tore at our ankles. Our anxiety argued they had merely been unnoticed earlier. Evening crickets, frogs and birds began to chant in unison. The forest became gray, the path slimmer. We entered a valley. The path disappeared, night darkness fell. We were lost.

Our hope seemed to lie in climbing one of the haystack hills for a view, but the plants were so thick and the slope so steep that we stopped halfway up. There on a slender ledge under a cliff, perched like birds, we spent the night.

A few crackers, several gulps of water, a poncho and wet clothes were our only supplies. We keenly wished we had had the foresight to bring a compass, a flashlight, heavier clothes and, above all, a topographical map with us. The hours moved at a sluggish pace as we tossed away rocks to construct narrow sleeping quarters, moved when an unidentified animal cracked twigs next to us, reconstructed sleeping quarters and constantly changed positions while keeping close to minimize shivering.

In retrospect the night was beautiful. The moon and stars luminesced in an otherwise black sky. Trees across the valley flapped silvery leaves. A mist settled in. Fireflies the size of nickels flickered by. Bats swooshed overhead. The rest of the world had disappeared.

Before dawn we slid down the hill and bushwhacked around the valley in search of an exit. We suddenly spied a sliver of plastic cup noticed the previous evening, proof we had relocated our trail. Our spirits revived when we rediscovered ferns, the red graffiti, the stream. After quenching our thirsts, we retraced our steps, this time trying a lower fork which for some reason had not looked right the day before. We passed the outcrops and within 15 minutes stepped onto the lumber road.

Early that morning several men from one of the camps, realizing we had not returned to our car, formed a search party and contacted the forest ranger, who found us walking along the road. In all the excitement, it was not until we were halfway back to San Juan that we remembered we never did reach the Río Tanamá.

Finding the Tanamá

About a year later I finally explored the Río Tanamá, on an expedition that involved rafting along a mile of the river. This time we started from behind the Arecibo Observatory, largest and most sophisticated radar/radio telescope in the world, and hiked through contrasting, primeval karst country, as remote and rugged as that seen in Río Abajo. Vines draped an old tobacco shed. Orchids the size of a baby's thumbnail grew on tree branches. Rubber plants and wild raspberries **(fresas),** delicious to eat, bordered the trail. A woman and her daughter washed clothes in a stream next to a small orchard of guava trees. This fruit, uncommonly high in vitamin C, is sold commercially as jelly, paste or nectar. Donkeys grazed in narrow pastures. Two men, then several women and children, peered at us from an unpainted shack far from any road. Next to the shack was a triangular corrugated metal shed, originally a hurricane shelter. A chicken coop perched on wooden legs. A dog slept under the house, two pigs lay in the yard, and laundry flapped on several lines.

The river was swift, shallow and the color of coffee. We inflated our boats, steered several unintended circles, then flowed with the current. For the most part the rafting was less than satisfactory. Innumerable rocks just below the surface banged knees and backbones. The boat was difficult to steer; it headed into one waterfall, then buckled, flipping us into a swirling pool that sucked us through a narrow crevasse. After that, we began to carry the boat through riverbank tangle on perilous stretches. And there was always the danger the river would rise suddenly — one high-water mark was nine feet above us — or that an accident would occur far from any means of help. A "normal" white-water river drops 10 to 15 feet to the mile; the Tanamá drops 86. In short, it is not an expedition I recommend, but the exotic beauty of the river is worth a brief description.

Tiers of haystack hills on either side of the river soon disappeared behind mossy canyon walls. The walls, dark and primeval, arch at the top as if they were once part of a cave which had collapsed. There is no ceiling; instead, forest is silhouetted against a strip of sky. Stalactites drip water, often from underground springs. Stalagmites in pocked grottoes resemble shrines and petrified dwarfs. Tree ferns and bright impatiens grow through cracks. Sandbars border curves in the river. In places the canyon narrows to 30 feet and rises to 100 (we never did see the 300-foot cliffs I had read about).

Just before we pulled the raft, battered hero of the day, out of the water for the last time, the river eases into a relatively deep natural canal. Bird chirps are magnified. Wet, moss green ledges extend from the walls. Streams cascade off the ledges and strike the river with tinkling sounds. Tree buttresses and plants spill over the top of the canyon and roots drape into the water. It is an extraordinary scene.

Below the canal the Tanamá enters a low, 300-yard-long cave in one of its most treacherous sections. We saved that for another day...

Branch patterns, Cambalache Forest

A. *Contemplating the Río Tanamá* B. *Teak leaves* C. *Sunset at Lago Guajataca*

1900s UPDATE: The karst forest reserves have changed little since the book was written. Guajataca (872-1045) has a new concrete and wood tower; its trails remain plentiful and maintained, and rangers still have a trail map. Cambalache (881-1004) will have swings again for children at its picnic site. Río Abajo (880-6557) has a rundown look, especially its picnic areas, and Road 621 is closed at its end to protect its new program for the propagation of endangered species. Forestry production, including a sawmill, post treatment plant, nursery and wood artisan shop, is now concentrated at one place, off Highway 10 south in Arecibo (881-1004, open weekdays). Fishing equipment can now be borrowed to fish along the banks of the Guajataca; see below. Camp Guajataka is available for rent on weekends; contact the Puerto Rico Council of Boy Scouts (767-0320). Call 868-2612 for the current observatory schedule. The section of the Río Tanamá I visited is still far off the beaten track, but roads are edging closer.

Resting in the Guajataca Forest

THE NATURAL RESOURCES AND ENVIRONMENTAL DEPART-MENT: This is a government agency which manages and protects the island's natural resources. Its Forest Service maintains the 14 Commonwealth reserves, which include coastal, karst and mountain forests. All reserves are open to the public daily from 7:00 a.m. to 4:00 p.m. Camping is permitted in many of the forests at designated sites; permits must be acquired beforehand. Check with the rangers at the forest stations about the current condition of the trails. In addition, DNR manages refuges at Mona, the bird-rich Humacao and Boquerón lagoons and Laguna Tortuguero; it provides fishing centers at Lago Guajataca and Lago Luchetti in Yauco; and oversees the beautiful, mile-long, lighthouse-topped Isla Caja de Muertos off Ponce. Call 724-3724 for more information. An excellent book about the forest trees is **Common Trees of Puerto Rico and the Virgin Islands**, by Elbert Little and Frank Wadsworth, available in English through the U.S. forest Service (766-5335) in Río Piedras.

Inside the Camuy cave, Tres Pueblos entrance

THE BIGGEST KARST JOURNEY
OF ALL -- INTO THE CAMUY

One of the largest caves in the Western world sprawls like a massive subway network beneath Puerto Rico's surface, yet unlike most subway lines, it is mysterious, fragile, dangerous — and little known to the public. This cave is named after the Río Camuy, which vanishes into the Blue Hole near Lares and tumbles through a collection of underground caverns, falls, siphons, lakes and chasms before it resurfaces four miles farther north. Several yawning sinkholes give local residents awesome peeks into the abyss, but most of the cave sits in perpetual darkness broken only by occasional flickers from the lamps of exploring speleologists.

Most visitors to the northern and western sections of the island are aware of the strange conical hills **(mogotes)** and rounded depressions **(abras)** that surround them. This is karst topography, which exists in few places in the Western world. The same forces that dissolve the limestone to produce these "haystack" hills and sinkholes are responsible for the dozens of caves that lie below Puerto Rico's surface, caves almost entirely undeveloped, some barely explored, a few still never seen by humans. And in this extensive underworld, where each cave is distinctive in its own right, none matches the Camuy system.

Descending into the depths

I first entered Camuy through the crater-shaped Tres Pueblos sinkhole (named for the municipalities of Hatillo, Camuy and Lares, whose boundaries converge here), a giant pit lined with teeming vegetation and sheer limestone cliffs and able to hold one and a third baseball fields or three El Morros. In its rich, moist soil a farmer once planted six and a half acres of plantains, somehow getting the fruit up a steep, muddy trail and a treacherous precipice to the top.

The Río Camuy emerges into the daylight of Tres Pueblos through a long toothy mouth of blackened rock, traverses the sinkhole, and returns underground through another cave entrance on the opposite side. To enter these apertures is to enter the dual lure of the twilight zone, a mingling of light and darkness, the known and the unknown. Outside, a circle of bright blue sky fringed by lush green forest beckons. Inside, shadows of conical stalactite groupings fade into tantalizing blackness. Soon even the bravest shafts of light and bits of moss vanish. One is alone in the rocks except for a sprinkling of spiders, worms, bugs, crabs and the kings of the cave, the bats, whose slippery droppings are vital to cave ecology.

A. *Ascending Tres Pueblos sinkhole* B. *Cave entrance, Tres Pueblos sinkhole* C. *Río Camuy, Tres Pueblos sinkhole*

Facts and history

Formed some five to 15 million years ago, the rocks were in turn formed into unadorned tunnels after the island surfaced above sea level. Following this, drip-formed calcite deposits began to decorate the tunnels with stalactite "icicles," stalagmite mounds and flowstone "tapestries."

What makes the Camuy system so outstanding? Several weeks after visiting the caves I questioned Norman Veve about this. Veve, dubbed the father of modern speleology in Puerto Rico — the first to maintain a serious interest in caves, to introduce professional techniques and equipment in island explorations, and to lecture about cave safety and conservation — mentioned four factors.

Camuy is a "macro" cave system: while not delicately beautiful, it is **big,** and unlike most caves maintains this bigness throughout its length. Six and half miles of cave have been probed, yet many unexplored leads remain. It has one of the largest known underground river systems in the world. Its accessible sinkhole entrances number among the biggest in the Western Hemisphere. And it is one of few major caves in the world so near a metropolitan area.

The Taino Indians, believing that the human race originated in caves, considered them sacred and ceremonial. They used Camuy for water supplies, carved petroglyphs on its walls, and explored, probably with torches, up to areas of deep water or steep drops.

While local residents had always been aware of cave-pocked sinkholes in their backyards, the caves remained largely unexplored until 1958, when a famous globe-trotting caver named Russell Gurnee began the systematic exploration of the Camuy system that would thrust Puerto Rico into the speleological limelight. Now no self-respecting cave explorer is unaware of the name Camuy.

The subterranean journey

Gurnee, who realized Camuy's potential for commercialization and conservation, proposed that the section of the cave which I was to visit — the half mile stretch from Tres Pueblos to La Ventosa blowhole — be developed for public recreation. While his plan remains merely that, another much smaller area of Camuy — the Empalme entrance — has been developed as a tourism and recreational complex by the Puerto Rican government.

My spelunking debut was made with 12 members of the Speleological Society of Puerto Rico. Many were dressed in jumpsuits decorated with badges; all came equipped with hard hats, life jackets, three light sources (carbide lamps for traditionalists, flashlights for the rest), boots and waterproofed food; most brought climbing hardware and gardening gloves. "This group is too big," fretted Arturo Torres, president of the society and leader of the day's expedition: four to six is the ideal size for ease of movement.

The society was formed in 1976 to promote speleology as both a science and a sport, to study and explore the island's caves in a controlled manner, and to protect the caves. An ambitious group with some 50 members and 23 committees, it seeks only serious initiates and does not seek excess publicity, which members fear could endanger both the caves and unprepared adventurers.

The potential for danger became evident soon after we entered the cave, bobbed across the tame, shallow river and climbed with sodden difficulty onto a jumble of boulders dubbed Mount Ararat after Gurnee's group waited out a flash flood there. Torres pointed his flashlight to the high water mark on the canyon wall, some 25 feet above the normal flow. "In a flash flood," Veve later added, "the water rises one foot a minute. You can actually watch it rise, and the river, full of flying branches, becomes an uncontrollable rage that is impossible to imagine if you have never seen it."

Two decades ago Héctor Bueso, an experienced cave explorer, underestimated the force of the flooded river at Mount Ararat and tried to cross it. The water's power ripped him from the safety rope and swept him through the sinkhole into the next cave. Only his life jacket was found, yet his spirit seems to remain in the cave as a warning, through the numerous recountings of his death, of the need for extreme caution.

As for the cave's fragility, I wondered how humans could possibly damage such a massive structure. "Caves are contained spaces," Veve explained, "that take an extremely long time to develop. What is most beautiful — the ornamentation — is also most fragile. For example, in the temperate zone it takes a stalactite one **century** to grow a cubic centimeter, the size of a sugar cube; here in the subtropics growth is only slighter faster. If some souvenir hunter decides to take home a lovely four-inch-long stalactite, he breaks off a millennium of work that is basically irreplaceable."

In addition, humans have been known to paint walls with graffiti, leave beer cans and wrappers, and dump wastes into the caves. The caves' essential beauty is their primordial, untouched quality; what society members fear are visitors who do not appreciate this concept.

Although a cave is merely an inert cavity devoid of light, the blackness creates an almost mystical aura in the mind, producing marvelous images. Life-jacketed bodies swimming up narrow canyons resemble clumsy waterbugs. Flickering lights seem part of a primeval religious procession. Columns become etched totem poles. Scalloped rimstone pools might be the abode of elves and fairies. Voices come from carbide flames instead of faces. Flowstones look like sheets of ice, stalagmites like melting ice cream, stalactites like tangled spaghetti. Yet always in the overwhelming darkness lurks the awareness that if something went wrong — a flooding river, a loss of light sources — this magic would suddenly turn into a stygian nightmare.

In our journey from Tres Pueblos to La Ventosa, we wandered through several impressive sections. The Espiral entrance, where half the group descended vertically, is a 300-foot cornucopia of rock. Streams of diffused light from its rim cast a cathedral-like beauty over the area. The Big Room — 200 feet wide and high, 600 feet long — dwarfed both hikers and light sources, but its immensity was hard to fathom in the darkness. Natural Bridge, a disorienting heap of pocked boulders, loose stones and mud, seemed inaptly named.

Torres and the other seasoned cavers led us around siphons (underwater passages), belayed us up 10-to-20-foot precipices, blew whistles to ensure we were together, and periodically shouted out support: "Todo bien? Everything okay?" We helped those next to us across rocks and down slippery slopes, and shined extra light at treacherous spots, aware of our total dependency on each other in this underground labyrinth.

Two and a half hours into the cave, we reached the Major Resurgence, an inauspicious pool set in a grotto where the Río Camuy reenters the main cavern. We could have continued upstream from this point, following the West Tributary as it enters the blackness toward places with such intriguing names as Igloo Waterfall, Magnetic Mud Passage and Hall of the White Maidens. Instead we set down soggy backpacks on a gravel bank; we took out crackers, sausages, nuts and longed for beer or hot rum toddies to warm shivering bodies. Then the primary purpose of the day's outing was started.

Camuy is a natural laboratory for scientists. Biologists can study the end results of the evolutionary process; geologists, the more than 100 vertical feet of exposed rock; hydrologists, the cave's complicated water flow. In addition, the society has expert cave photographers, cartographers, scuba divers, geographers, climbers, engineers and attorneys.

The day's plan was for several scuba divers to explore the yard-wide Resurgence Passage, an underwater tunnel, which possibly leads to another cavern never before found by humans. Divers took turns inching into the murky black water, an aluminum air tank strapped to a backpack, a flashlight in one hand, a safety rope in the other.

Some seven feet beyond the opening, the hole was choked with limbs and tree trunks. More than a dozen logs were pulled out, relay fashion, but the hole remained choked and seemed to angle downward, an indication it would not soon reach dry land.

This meant another expedition, bringing bigger, heavier tanks, an almost impossible task along the Tres Pueblos route. Much nearer is La Ventosa entrance, but it involves some 400 feet of difficult free fall descent. In spite of our failure to find a new cavern to claim and name, no one felt very disappointed, for we had explored an underwater passage, increased our knowledge about Camuy and discovered, or rediscovered, an impressive half mile of baroque tunnel.

Caving

This thrill of discovery and rediscovery is what Veve stressed when asked why he became addicted to caving. In 1956 he visited his first cave, Aguas Buenas, with a friend; they were unprepared and got lost. While this experience soured his friend to caving, it whetted Veve's interest

Entering the Camuy cave (Photo by John Harmon)

and he began to read all available books about speleology. Initially, fellow enthusiasts were scarce; some of the first were Veve's UPR students, whose interest in grades may have outweighed their cave interests. Now a part of him — his "loner" side — misses those small, informal trips.

Veve mentioned other joys of caving: the adventure, the insignificance of worries once inside such massiveness, the total silence and absolute darkness — primitive, almost womblike conditions rarely experienced by adults. A member of our Tres Pueblos expedition added that caving challenges had given him greater confidence in himself. A strong camaraderie, which I noticed from the early morning drive out until the beer and tacos dinner later that night, also keeps cavers coming back.

Did Veve have any regrets after 26 years of caving? Yes, two. One was that he never wrote down his pioneer experiences in this now internationally known cave system. The other was that caving is such a physical sport, a combination of hiking, swimming, climbing, leaping, sliding; there are sections of the cave he would like to see again but cannot because of a bad knee.

Since Gurnee first peered into Camuy in 1958, a lot has happened: the cave became famous, Veve found solitude, Bueso died, the Speleological Society of Puerto Rico was formed, many caverns got their first look at humans, society members gained confidence; and during that time the cave formations — those exquisite, immutable structures — have grown a mere quarter cubic centimeter.

1990s UPDATE: With the opening of the Río Camuy Cave Park (Road 129, km. 19.8), the Camuy system of caves is now well known to the public, which has flocked to the park. The Empalme entrance and Cueva Clara have been beautifully developed; visitors reach the 400-foot-deep Empalme by taking a trolley into a smaller sinkhole and walking through the cave. A trolley also takes visitors to platforms overlooking Tres Pueblos sinkhole and a stairway descending to the Espiral entrance of the caves. Call 898-3100 for current information. There are now tours for the adventurous (and hardy) to explore undeveloped sections of Camuy and other island caves; Aventuras Tierra Adentro (788-5461) has experienced guides trained in cave rescue who are members of the Island's Speleological Society. The Blue Hole (where the Camuy vanishes underground) is visible off Road 134 south of Arecibo. A wonderful adventure book, **Discovery at Río Camuy** by Russell and Jeanne Gurnee, is usually available (in Spanish) at the park. Those interested in immersing themselves into the science of caving should contact La Sociedad Espeleológica de Puerto Rico, Apto. 31074, 65th Inf. Station, Río Piedras, P.R. 00929.

Playa Kahlua near Manatí

THE SEARCH FOR A
SECRET BEACH

Most people would like to discover their own secret beach — something with palms, pristine sand, perhaps a cove, certainly no other people. Fewer people realize that the search for such a beach can be as pleasurable as the discovery itself.

Beaches that did not tempt us

The beaches immediately west of San Juan did not entice us the day we went in search of a secret beach along Puerto Rico's northern coast. The beach around the bay at Boca Vieja has a long, gentle curve, but the Cataño factories in the background, numerous cars beside the road and an almost licorice color to the water detracted from the lovely shape. Past Punta Salinas, site of a newly renovated public bathing resort, the water turns a dark blue. Skeletons of fishing piers and shady wooden gazebos called **bohíos** line gray sand. A stretch of reef makes swimming difficult. The drive is pleasant, though, with the ocean on one side and sugar cane fields, hills and tropical vegetation on the other.

In Dorado, a town of brightly painted murals, the main street is often jammed with beachgoers. Playa de Dorado at the end of town is another public bathing resort, with restrooms, lifeguards and picnic areas scattered along the beach. The main road curves to the west through a cool, tree canopied stretch between the Dorado Beach and Cerromar Beach hotels. Pastel flowers brighten the foliage, and pink oleander bushes hide fences. Such elegance also did not attract us that day; we were in search of more rugged beauty. Beyond the Cerromar Beach Hotel and several seafood restaurants is a third public bathing resort called Playa Cerro Gordo. To its right a mound of rock topped with tangled vegetation juts into the sea.

Here the road ends. Those who want to continue along the coast must temporarily backtrack to Highway 2. A number of interesting scenes line the backtracking roads, including a nursery, a huge corrugated metal building where mushrooms were once grown, the ruins of the San Vicente sugar refinery and rice fields planted on former sugar cane land.

Semi-secret beaches

The water at Playa de Vega Baja, next stop along the coast, was clear, calm and turquoise in color the summer day we visited it (during the winter the Atlantic tends to be much rougher). A seawall separates homes from the small bay. Several benches on a boardwalk face the sea. A concrete ramp angles into the water, where several boats remain moored during calm weather. No trees border the sand.

Large beach rocks arc into the sea from the beach. The rocks protect the bay and a shallow sea pool. These rocks are actually cemented sand dunes. Ten thousand years ago the sea level was as much as 300 feet lower than it is now. Later, loose sand dunes became cemented together, forming reefs and rocky islets along the northern coast. Depending on the viewer, the rocks resemble sleeping dinosaurs, prehistoric carapaces or moon craters. Visitors scramble over them to fish or view the sea. Unfortunately, people also use them to stash litter and declare love (e.g., **Carlos y María** printed in paint).

Although the beach is picturesque, its lack of shade (there is one large shelter) and the foreboding arrival of many cars at an early hour kept us moving westward. The road passes a numbered wall that was once a shooting range for the National Guard, and several fields where cows roamed under palms.

Punta Chivato is behind an abandoned National Guard airstrip which may be converted into a recreational area under a development plan called Project Tortorico. A few local residents were parked in groups along the asphalt, surrounded by many crushed cans. The point is secluded, rugged, and unsuitable for swimming: flat, pocked sand rocks and reef extend from low-lying thicket well into the sea. Vegetation is a dry tangle of seagrapes, flowering **alelí** and waxy plants. Several types of fish inhabit the reef. A patch of field showed signs of recent camping.

Playa Tortuguero curves for a mile along the road. The sea that day was translucent and calm, although an undertow pulled slightly. Los Tubos, a surfing beach with rideable waves most of the year, is at the eastern end of the beach. Several abandoned buildings, one with a bright sun painted on its wall, identify the spot. Massive boulders sprouting vegetation border the beach to the west. Hidden on the edge of the boulders is a disfigured palm tree shaped like a rocking horse which makes a fine seat from which to contemplate the sea spraying against rocks 20 feet below. The beach's accesibility to the road ruled it out as secluded. Before continuing our beach search, we explored the adjacent Laguna Tortuguero.

Laguna Tortuguero

Laguna Tortuguero is the larger of two freshwater lagoons on the island (the other, Laguna Cartagena, is in the southwest). Although only several hundred feet from the coast, it is fed by underground springs and has no natural opening to the sea. In 1940 the Army built a drainage canal connecting the lagoon to the ocean (apparently to alleviate flooding and a bad mosquito problem), which accounts for the slight salinity of the water. The three-mile-long, half-mile-wide and four-foot-deep lagoon was named after its small community of native turtles.

Palm trees and grasses border Tortuguero to the north, forests and sand to the south. Along the water's edge are marshes of typha grass with numerous cattails. Jeep roads and paths skirt the lagoon near the beach. Men are often seen collecting coconuts here. Shade from trees and vines relieves the mugginess only slightly. There are dozens of ferns and a few pterocarpus **(palo de pollo)** trees, recognized by high, thin buttresses curving snakelike along the ground. Across the lagoon are pastures and patches of silica sand (used in making glass) which feels like talcum power. No houses surround the lagoon.

The setting seems uncharacteristic of Puerto Rico. One scientist said that, except for the haystack hills in the background, it reminded him of the Florida Everglades. The slate color of the water, rippling in the wind, reminded me of even colder country.

In addition to its lovely tranquillity, Laguna Tortuguero is important for its diverse soils and vegetation. The intermingling of marshes, grasses, Australian pine forest, karst terrain and sand has produced several distinctions. This is botanically the richest area for its size under the U.S. flag. Two species of carnivorous plants eat insects. Of 13 orchid species, one grows nowhere else in the world. Seven species of birds and waterfowl have been declared rare or endangered. A tiny community of spectacle caimans (alligators) up to five feet long normally keep out of the way of visitors. Sea shells have been found on the bottom of the lagoon; how they got there remains a mystery.

Near the entrance to the Puerto Rico National Guard facilities (constructed for use during World War II and still maintained) local fishermen slip rowboats into the lagoon. Limited fishing is permitted; the fish are small and include varieties of eel and snapper. Some visitors swim here; the possibility of bilharzia-carrying snails in the water keeps others out.

Several years ago environmentalists won a battle to stop a construction materials company from dynamiting and possibly dredging part of the lagoon. Currently, there are plans for a different kind of development which would make Laguna Tortuguero into a nature reserve and center for recreation and scientific investigation.

A. *Coastal pasture near Vega Baja* B. *Waves breaking at Punta Chivato*

Discovering the secret beach

Several large grottoes, blackened by picnic fires, provide unique shelters on the road behind jewel-like Mar Chiquita, some five miles west of Playa Tortuguero. A tiny bay fans into the coast; two sets of dune rocks close off all but a funnel of water from the sea. The bay is usually calm and crystalline.

There is something for everyone at Mar Chiquita. As at Vega Baja, fishermen and sea-watchers roam the jagged rocks. Waders use a shallow inlet. Snorkelers circle pieces of coral. Surfers ride the surges of water between the rocks, and divers leap from the ledges. Algae-covered reef in the water doubles as a slide.

Next to the bay, isolated palms and Indian almond trees shade the sand. Food vans provide drinks and snacks on weekends, but there are no other facilities. Mar Chiquita may be little known to the residents of San Juan, but it is well known to the residents of nearby Manatí. Crowds jammed into the bay the day we were there, one of the most popular beach holidays of the year, yet a mile of wide beach to the east was practically deserted. We walked in that direction.

Cliffs covered with seagrapes rise at the edge of the sand. Reefs extend into the sea. A small forest of palms, vines and chunky boulders looks like the entrance to some lost kingdom.

Beyond the forest the sand widens into a beach bordered on both sides by rocks. Here we found our "secret" beach. The sea bottom is sandy. Brisk waves pull the clear water back and forth. Palms, almond trees and seagrapes sprout in pale sand. When we sat against a palm tree to watch its plumes brush against the stark blue sky, a bed of red ants immediately ejected us, but that was the site's sole imperfection. Best of all, only four other people shared this sea sanctuary with us.

Later we decided such a beach merited a name, and toyed with Playa Jacuzzi, Playa de las Palmas Inclinadas (beach of the sloping palms) and Playa Apacible (placid beach). Much later, a local resident wrote that he and his friends had dubbed the site Playa Kahlua and made T-shirts with the beach's name on it. Playa Kahlua may not be so secret after all, but it will seem so to most visitors.

Beach vegetation, Playa Tortuguero

A. *Playa de Vega Baja* B. A *"bouquet"* of tree limbs, road near Manatí C. *Laguna Tortuguero*

1990s UPDATE: Take a detailed highway map and follow the coastal roads from Cataño to Mar Chiquita in Manatí (off road 685; ask). A dirt off Road 687 leads to Laguna Tortuguero's small beach. Tortuguero is now classified as a wildlife refuge (see the Karst Country article); no one seems to know what happened to Project Tortorico. Like many north coast beaches areas, Mar Chiquita is now bordered by new housing developments. Playa Kahlua is about a mile east of Mar Chiquita. Lock your car well in this area. Los Tubos Beach (off Road 686) hosts a well-attended beach festival every summer; otherwise, these beaches are primarily used by local residents.

A NOTE ABOUT PUERTO RICO'S BALNEARIOS: Those who do not mind weekend and holiday crowds should try the public bathing beaches (**balnearios**), where there are safe swimming areas and places to shower and change. Public beaches are located at lovely settings around the island (see **Qué Pasa**'s center map); the best-known one is still Luquillo Beach. Several beaches have tent sites while others have trailer sites and cabins for rent. For more information contact the Department of Recreation and Sports at 722-1551.

Palm trunk seat near Playa Tortuguero

The other Puerto Rico
INDEX

Shaded page numbers refer to notes about the subject that precedes the number.

S

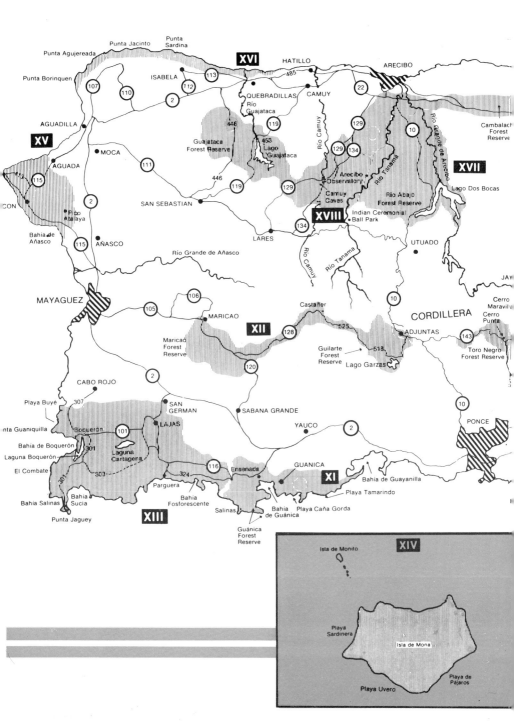

to Rico

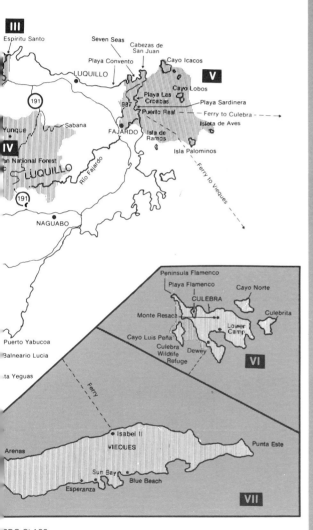

RDO CLASS

ATLANTIC OCEAN

Playa Tortuguero
Punta Chivato
Playa de Vega Baja
Playa Cerro Gordo
Playa Mar Chiquita
Playa de Dorado
Ensenada de Boca Vieja
Punta Salinas
SAN JUAN
Boca de Cangrejos
Laguna Torrecilla
Playa Vacia Ta
PIÑONES

685
686
688
693
DORADO
165
165
187
II
LOIZ

XIX
TOA BAJA
CATAÑO
Laguna de Piñones
Piñones Forest Reserve

VEGA BAJA
2
22
Laguna San José
CAROLINA

MANATI
Laguna Tortuguero

149
167
BAYAMON
I
3
Botanical Garden UPR Experimental Station
Río Grande de Loiza

CIALES
52
185

NARANJITO
1

167

X
OROCOVIS
IX
Cañón San Cristóbal
Río de la Plata
CAGUAS
SIERRA

149
Río Saliente
Lago Matrullas
156
COMERIO
30

CENTRAL
BARRANQUITAS
Ruta Panorámica
Río Usabón
52

143
JYA

162
AIBONITO
14
184
Carite Forest Reserve
Cerro La Santa
Ruta Panorámica

Divisoria
151
CAYEY
Lago Carite

Lago Guineo
VILLALBA
Embalse Toa Vaca
COAMO
184
181
VIII
182

Cerro ayuya
Río Inabón
Lago Guayabal
JUANA DIAZ
14
179
Río Grande de Patillas
MAUNABO
3

52
15
PATILLAS

1
52
52
GUAYAMA
3
Pu
Playa Mau

SALINAS
Central Aguirre

a Caja de Muertos

CARIBBEAN SEA
Bahia de Jobos
Jobos National Estuarine Sanctuary

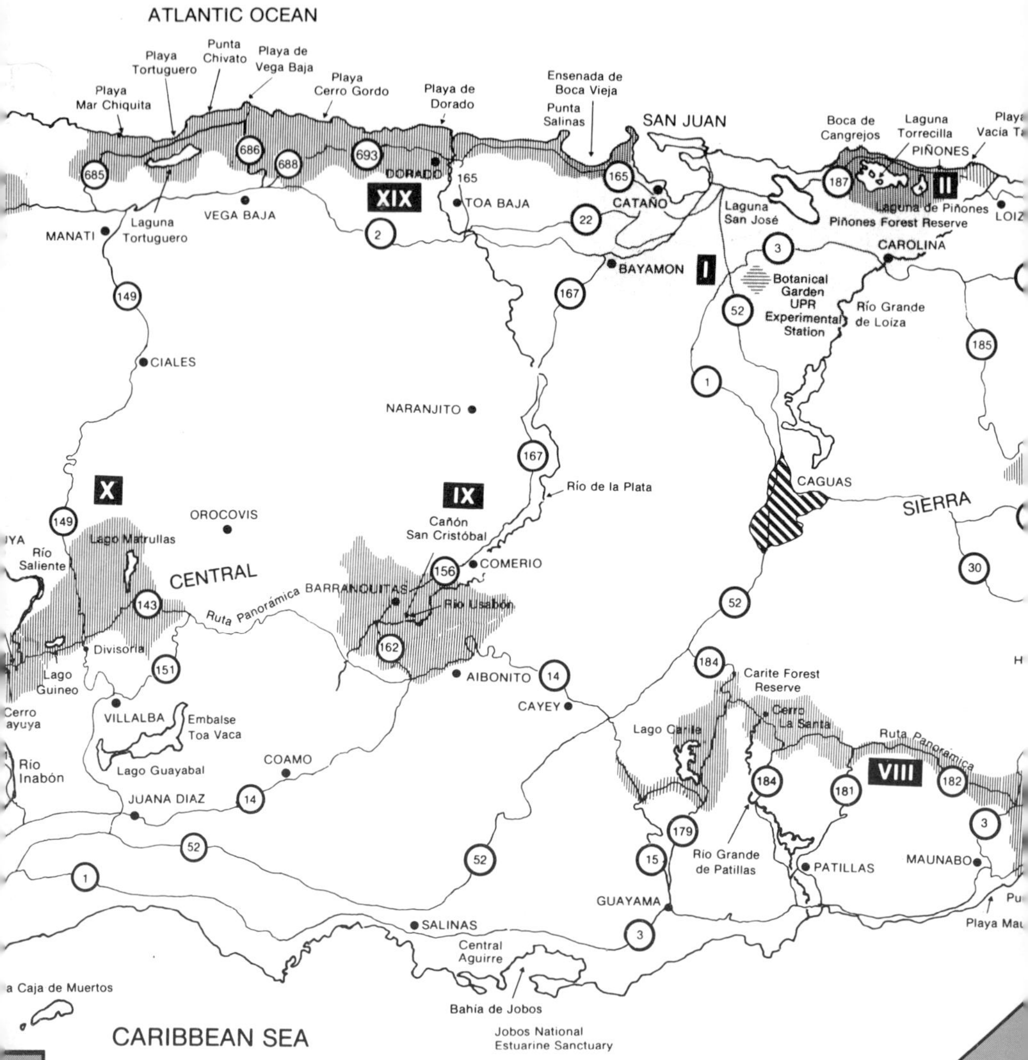

MAP ILLUSTRATION